Railway Memories No.21

ROTHERHAM MEXBOROUGH & WATH

Adrian Booth & Stephen Chapman

BELLCODE BOOKS
21 DALE AVENUE
TODMORDEN
WEST YORKSHIRE OL14 6BA
email: bellcode4books@yahoo.co.uk

Visiting ex-Midland Railway 4F 0-6-0 No. 43953 looks rather resplendent outside Canklow shed in 1965.
The Workington-based loco was there to work the 4F Farewell railtour of South Yorkshire and East Midlands branches. *Tom Greaves*

Copyright © 2009 Bellcode Books
ISBN 9781871233 21 6

Edited by Steve Chapman

Printed in the UK by the Amadeus Press, Ltd., Cleckheaton, West Yorkshire.

FRONT COVER: Iron ore trains between the East Midlands and both local and more distant steel plants were a notable feature of freight operations in the area. York 9F 2-10-0 No. 92205 passes beneath the magnificent semaphore gantry at Masborough South Junction on 23rd August 1964 with empty ore tipplers returning, in all probability, from Teesside. *Adrian Booth*

BACK COVER TOP: A Class EM1 electric loco on a passenger train at Wath Yard. No. E26021 had just taken over the Locomotive Club of Great Britain's Great Central Rail Tour of 3rd September 1966 from a pair of B1 4-6-0s. Judging by the Southern Region green coaches, the train could be formed of a York-Bournemouth set. *Jack Wild*

BACK COVER BOTTOM: Trolley buses, one green Mexborough & Swinton and one blue Rotherham Corporation, wait at Denaby crossing as WD 2-8-0 No. 90486 thunders by with westbound mineral empties in March 1961. *Geoff Warnes/ Colour-Rail BRE1772*

FRONTISPIECE: It is the late 1940s and the railways have just been nationalized. Still displaying its LMS number 1066 but with "British Railways" on the tender, Canklow(19C)-based Compound 4-4-0 No.1066 calls at Rotherham Masborough with a Sheffield-bound local. Within a year or two, this engine would be transferred across the Pennines to Trafford Park. *Tom Greaves*

Our thanks are due to all those people who have so willingly provided material and assistance for this edition of Railway Memories. We would especially like to thank Robert Anderson, Ron Hollier and the staff of Rotherham Archive and Local Studies. **Information for this book** about the 1950s and later has come mainly from original sources, especially British Railways documents, but for historical information, acknowledgement is due to the following sources: The History of the British Coal Industry before 1700 by John Hatcher(Oxford University Press,) A Regional History of the Railways of Great Britain, South & West Yorkshire by David Joy(David & Charles,) Railways of the South Yorkshire Coalfield from 1880 by A.L. Barnett(RCTS,) The Light Railway King of the North by A.L. Barnett(The Railway & Canal Historical Society,) contemporary editions of Modern Railways, Railway Magazine, Railway World and Trains Illustrated.

INTRODUCTION

This edition of Railway Memories begins with a brain-teaser. Which town once had three railway stations, all of them closed but one remains open? The answer, of course, is Rotherham.

Of those three stations, two hosted long-distance expresses and one of them even trains between London and Scotland, but now Rotherham's one station is served only by local, if frequent, services.

Wath-upon-Dearne also once had three stations on three different routes, a marshalling yard and a modern locomotive depot - now it has no railway at all. Mexborough still has its station but everything else, including the large steam loco depot, is long gone.

Coal, steel and general heavy industry ensured that, but for the loss of some passenger services and stations, the railways of the Don and Dearne valleys survived almost intact into the modern era. Substantial closures did not really take place until the 1980s when economic recession, industrial decline and colliery closures took their toll. Consequently, the diesel era is well represented within these pages because the 1970s and 80s behold scenes which are themselves now just memories.

Thankfully, the area is still alive with railway activity but passenger and freight trains mostly pass through with barely a glance, the many sidings, depots and industrial plants that dominated the scene having

Contents

Page 4   Setting the scene

Page 30   The Midland

Page 62   The GC Rotherham-Conisbrough

Page 80   Mexborough-Wath-Penistone

Page 101   The Dearne Valley Railway

Page 104   The South Yorkshire Joint

Page 109   Industrials

virtually all disappeared into the mists of time.

On 7th September 1964 British Railways began using the 24-hour clock in its working timetables so we use am and pm up to that date and thereafter the 24-hour clock except where direct comparisons are made between times in different eras.

Leaving Mexborough motive power depot behind it, Robinson Great Central-design O4/3 2-8-0 No. 63656, of a variant introduced in 1917 for the Railway Operating Division, passes the closed Swinton station on the GC line to Sheffield with a Down mineral train at 2.55pm on 13th May 1961.
John Beaumont/Robert Anderson archive

SETTING THE SCENE

If proof were needed that parallel worlds exist then the railways around Rotherham and Mexborough were, in a sense, just that. Traditionally they have consisted of two distinct systems which shadow each other - the lines of the old Midland Railway and those of the Great Central Railway.

For their entire length these companies' lines through the Rotherham area were bordered on each side by large steel works, collieries, coke plants. scrap yards and heavy industrial premises of all kinds, most with their attendant private sidings. Views from carriage windows were far from pretty but for some of us were fascinating in the extreme.

Rotherham, Mexborough and Wath-upon-Dearne sit in a geographical area of coal measures bordered immediately to the east by an upfold of magnesian limestone rising to 425ft above sea level near Silverwood to form a barrier with Doncaster and the level, formerly marshy ground leading eastwards to the Humber estuary. To the west, are the Pennine foothills formed of millstone grits while cutting between these flanks of higher ground are the two main river valleys - the Don(originally known as the Dun) which flows south to north east, and its tributary the Dearne flowing west to east, the confluence of the two being at Conisbrough(note the remarkable similarity between the river names.) It was these valleys that the early - and principal - railways mostly followed.

Coal is known to have been mined an area bounded by the Don and Dearne valleys since medieval times. Outcrops of the Barnsley, Silkstone and Parkgate seams made it easy to reach by early means. Around Rotherham, coal measures were exposed to the surface by faults and erosion. Iron-making goes back possibly to pre-Roman times. As the industrial revolution dawned in the mid-18th century and with iron ore, limestone and charcoal from the densely wooded slopes all readily available, the craft grew into the giant industry for which the region became renowned. As coke replaced charcoal for fuelling ever bigger furnaces, the demand for coal grew rapidly and mining with it, not to mention the number of coke ovens.

Early wooden tramroads using wagons powered by men or horses were used in the 18th century to move coal between mines and waterways for onward transport to Rotherham and Sheffield. Among the first, dating from the mid-1700s was a half-mile line from pits near Bassingthorpe to Masborough (Masbrough as it was then) where it met the new Rotherham Cut of the River Don navigation. Another ran from Earl Fitzwilliam's pits at Higher Stubbin and Swallow Wood to his Greasbrough canal which carried the coal to the River Don which in turn took it on to Rotherham and Sheffield.

These were short, isolated tracks serving only their owners. The first public main line railways came between 1838 and 1840. The North Midland Railway, promoted by George Hudson, was building its Derby to Leeds line through Masborough, Kilnhurst, Swinton and on to Leeds via Cudworth and Normanton where there was to be a junction with the York & North Midland Railway to York. Hudson vowed to "mek all't railways come t' York" but even the Railway King couldn't persuade his engineer, George Stephenson, to mek them come

t' Sheffield. The line by-passed the then fledgling industrial town, following the level lower Don Valley from Masborough southwards through Treeton, Killamarsh, Barrow Hill and Chesterfield because Stephenson considered the hilly terrain south of Sheffield would make the line too steeply graded for the locomotives then available and too expensive to build.

Sheffield's civic leaders and industrialists who could see their own town's growth being stunted by the lack of a railway, were determined not to be left out in the cold. But for them too, the terrain south of Sheffield was too formidable so they went north and tapped into the North Midland by promoting the 5.25-mile Sheffield & Rotherham Railway. Completed on 1st November 1838 - the first railway in both towns - it ran to its own terminus at Westgate in Rotherham town centre and, pre-dating the North Midland by 18 months it was, at the time, another isolated line. The NMR built a two-mile goods line from the S&R at Holmes through Masborough to Earl Fitzwilliam's Greasbrough colliery line at Parkgate, which it opened on 10th August 1838 and leased to the S&R. Running alongside the Masborough-Leeds line for most of its length, it enabled coal to be moved by rail throughout to Sheffield. The main line opened between Masborough and Derby on 11th May 1840 and between Masborough and Leeds on 1st July.

Completion of the North Midland line meant that Rotherham with its station at Masborough, was blessed from the start with services to York, Leeds, the Midlands and London. While, of course, Sheffield was not left out. The S&R opened the short Holmes-Masborough section of its Greasbrough branch to passengers and through carriages were conveyed by NMR trains to all the same destinations as those enjoyed by Rotherham. By 1845 when the S&R was absorbed into the Midland Railway(the NMR's successor) five major iron and steel companies had established premises along the route of the S&R.

More than nine years were to pass before another main line railway entered the scene when on 10th November 1849, the South Yorkshire Railway opened its 8-mile line from Doncaster to a Rotherham-facing junction with the Midland at Swinton. Two months later the railway junction at Mexborough was founded when a single line was laid westwards, passing underneath the Derby-Leeds line and past Wath-upon-Dearne to a goods terminus at Earl Fitzwilliam's Elsecar ironworks, the line opening on 1st February 1850. Here, Fitzwilliam, chairman of the SYR at the time, had his own platform. On 1st July the following year a line from Elsecar Junction, Wath, through Wombwell to Barnsley was opened, the stretch to Mexborough doubled and a Barnsley-Mexborough-Doncaster passenger service introduced by the Great Northern Railway.

All new lines built in the area over the next 23 years were connected with the South Yorkshire Railway. First, completed by April 1852 was another purely goods line, 6.5 miles from Aldam Junction, Wombwell, to Moor End, serving collieries on what was destined to become the Worsborough branch. In September 1854 a company with the somewhat exhausting title of Sheffield, Rotherham, Barnsley, Wakefield, Huddersfield &

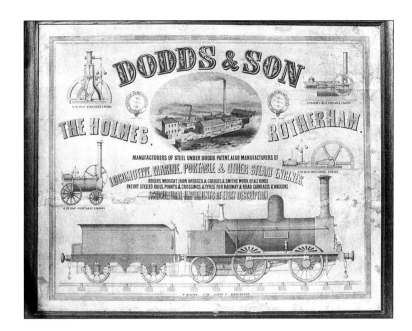

The Sheffield & Rotherham Railway's consulting engineer was Isaac Dodds who owned the Holmes engine works in Rotherham. Although this Dodds poster depicts an 0-4-2 locomotive *Indian*, the first locomotives supplied to the S&R, *Victory, London, Leeds, Agilis* and *Rotherham*, were built elsewhere. *Adrian Booth collection*

Goole opened its line from Aldam Junction to Blackburn Valley, just north of Sheffield(nowadays next-door to the Meadow Hall shopping centre) where it initially joined the Midland line. This created the first through route between Doncaster, Mexborough and Sheffield, although it did miss Rotherham. It also enabled a Barnsley-Sheffield passenger service though trains had to reverse at Aldam Junction which faced Mexborough until 1879 when a Barnsley-facing curve was installed.

Between 1863 and April 1871 the South Yorkshire extended its lines into Sheffield with the stage-by-stage opening of the Mexborough-Rotherham-Tinsley-Sheffield (Woodburn Junction) line, passenger services commencing on 3rd April, three weeks after goods traffic. The line was built without Act of Parliament because the SY owned most of the land but this meant that the Midland Railway was under no obligation to provide a bridge for it to pass under its main line just south of Masborough. The line's builders got round this by using the existing canal bridge, the SY already owning the canal. They diverted the canal via the river and provided a formation for the railway by sinking barges loaded with stone in the old cut. Another engineering challenge which delayed the line's completion while more money was found, was the need to provide a swing bridge over the Greasbrough Canal at Parkgate. On 1st June 1874 a south-west spur from Mexborough No.3 to Mexborough No.1 was completed, enabling goods trains to run directly between Sheffield, Rotherham, Wath and Barnsley.

The South Yorkshire Railway was an independent company with agreements for various others to operate trains over its metals but in 1874 it was absorbed into the Manchester, Sheffield and Lincolnshire Railway which had in 1845 opened the Manchester-Sheffield line over the Pennines via Woodhead and Penistone, and which in 1899 renamed itself the Great Central upon completing its extension to London Marylebone.

May 1879 saw the addition of another major route into the area, a line owned by the Midland and North Eastern railways intended to provide a more direct route for increasing volumes of traffic between Sheffield, York and the North East avoiding the increasingly congested North Midland line. This was the Swinton & Knottingley Joint which headed north towards Moorthorpe, Pontefract and Ferrybridge from a junction with the Midland line at Wath Road, Swinton. It included a spur from Mexborough West to Dearne Junction providing the MS&L, which was granted running powers, with access. The S&K became the principal route for long distance expresses between the North East and the West Country.

The MS&L completed a short but very significant section of line on 2nd August 1880 when it filled the 2.5-mile gap between the western extremity of the South Yorkshire line at Wentworth Colliery and West Silkstone Junction where it joined the Barnsley-Penistone line. This created a direct route via Woodhead for the increasing volume of coal being carried to mills and factories in Lancashire from the many pits around Barnsley and Rotherham. But this short distance demanded a 200ft climb up from the Wentworth Valley to reach Penistone, requiring the fearsome 1 in 40 Worsborough Bank despite major earthworks to minimize the gradient. Two years later, a three quarter mile spur from the S&K at Dearne Junction to Wath Junction was opened.

Upon opening of the Hull & Barnsley Railway in 1885, the owners of Denaby and Cadeby collieries at Conisbrough sought an alternative route to Hull and so promoted the South Yorkshire Junction Railway which ran northwards from the Doncaster-Mexborough line at Lowfield Junction to Wrangbrook where it joined the H&B main line. Opened in 1894, it was operated by the H&B but remained an entirely independent company until taken over by the LNER in 1924. It also carried a short-lived passenger service. See Railway Memories No.12 for more about this line.The rail network in the Dearne and Don valleys was now as good as complete but 20 years later a new round of building would begin. Mining techniques

With the former S&R line to Rotherham Westgate passing underneath in the foreground, Brush Type 2s Nos. D5813 and D5670 approach Rotherham Masborough on the 'Old Road' with a class 8 mineral train on 27th January 1968. The second bridge carries the line over a navigable cut of the River Don and, since 1987, the Holmes chord linking the GC line to the Midland. *Adrian Booth*

and equipment were advancing rapidly by this time and with the start of the 20th century much deeper and richer coal seems east of Rotherham and Mexborough were being exploited in what became known as the concealed or buried coalfield. Big mines with output levels hitherto unknown were being sunk and the mine owners would need the coal moving to their markets. This led to an unseemly scramble by the railway companies and entrepreneurs as they fought to win this lucrative new business. A complex tangle of competing schemes for new lines emerged, alliances were formed and broken, schemes were promoted and thrown out by Parliament, but a few became reality, usually in a different form to that originally promoted and mostly as joint lines.

The first new line of the 20th century was the Hull & South Yorkshire Extension Railway which ran eight miles to Wath from the Hull & Barnsley Railway's main line at Wrangbrook. Dropping under the North Midland on a 1 in 115 gradient, it terminated at right angles to the Mexborough-Barnsley line, on the north side, just across the road from the GC's Wath station. Although carrying a passenger service, its main function was to serve the collieries at Hickleton, Wath and Manvers. It opened in 1902, four years after being taken over by the H&B. See Railway Memories No.12 for more.

Coal traffic across the Pennines via Wath and the GC's Woodhead line had reached a critical level and major new investment was needed in order to deal with it efficiently. It is said there were 45 pits within 10 miles of Wath and the GC chose this location for a major new marshalling yard that would gather together loads from over 100 Yorkshire pits and form them into trains for onward delivery, mostly across the Pennines. Fully opened on 4th December 1907, Wath Yard was the country's first power-operated gravitation hump yard. Over a mile long, it was situated on the south side of the Mexborough-Barnsley line. Designed to handle 5000 wagons every 24 hours, it had eight eastbound reception roads and 31 departure sidings, and nine westbound reception roads with 31 departure sidings while the total number of sidings was 110. The Mexborough-Wath line was quadrupled and the layout at Wombwell remodelled so that coal trains from the Barnsley direction could work direct to Penistone. Four giant 0-8-4 tank engines were built for the GC by Beyer Peacock of Manchester for hump shunting, and two more by the London & North Eastern Railway, the GC's successor from 1923. The yard also despatched trains to Grimsby for fuelling trawlers and to Immingham for shipping.

By the late 19th century coal exports were becoming big business and several Dearne Valley colliery owners concluded that they urgently needed improved links to the Humber ports. With little satisfaction from the existing railway companies to this end, they promoted the Dearne Valley Railway which via its western end connected pits at Grimethorpe, Houghton, Hickleton, Goldthorpe, Barnburgh, Denaby and Cadeby with the H&B main line giving direct access to Hull, while at the eastern end it joined the Great Northern in the Doncaster area which provided access to both London and the Great Central's new deep water port at Immingham. It also had powers to build a dock on the River Don at Mexborough. The DV was completed in stages between March 1902 and October 1908, the final stretch between Cadeby Colliery, Conisbrough, and Doncaster's Black Carr Junction being the most demanding in civil engineering terms. Not only did the DV necessitate a 1 in 100 ruling gradient throughout most of its length, it had to negotiate the limestone hills east of Conisbrough through a 70ft deep cutting and cross the Don valley at Conisbrough by an awesome viaduct standing 113ft above the river with 21 arches and a 150ft central span. The Lancashire & Yorkshire Railway, which had a major stake in the DV, built its own line from Shafton Junction where the DV joined the H&B, to Crofton, near Wakefield, thus connecting the DV with the port of Goole and destinations across the Pennines. It was the L&Y which was chosen to operate the DV and which eventually took it over, adding a passenger service between Wakefield Kirkgate and Edlington, on the outskirts of Doncaster, in 1912.

East of Rotherham, some sort of order eventually emerged from the various competing schemes and work got under way to bring railways to new deep pits at such places as Dinnington, Thurcroft, Maltby and Silverwood. One of the first to be completed was the Roundwood & Dalton Colliery Railway, an internal colliery line built to connect Silverwood Colliery with the Great Central and Midland lines north of Rotherham at Roundwood. It incorporated an existing colliery line which already connected these main lines and a basin on the River Don with Roundwood Colliery. Opened in time for the start of production at Silverwood in 1904, it required a substantial double track girder bridge over the Don and a 1 in 47 climb up to Silverwood. The Shireoaks, Laughton & Maltby Railway, a joint venture by the rival Midland and Great Central companies, was opened for goods between Brantcliffe Junction(Brancliffe from 1908,) west of Worksop on the Great Central line from Sheffield, and Dinnington on 2nd October 1905.

Meanwhile, three more companies, the North Eastern, the L&Y and the Great Northern, had joined with the Midland and GC to form the South Yorkshire Joint Railway which, incorporating the Laughton-Maltby section of the SL&M, was authorized by Parliament in 1903.

The mostly single track, running from Dinnington & Laughton to the GC's Doncaster-Grimsby line at Kirk Sandall with various connections into other lines south of Doncaster, and including a branch to Dinnington Colliery, opened officially for goods on 1st January 1909, the L&Y working coal trains from late 1908. A Shireoaks-Doncaster passenger service was introduced on 1st December 1910. In 1911 a short branch was added to serve Maltby Colliery. Also by October 1909, other lines connecting Thrybergh and Silverwood with the South Yorkshire Joint at Anston Junction plus a goods branch from Braithwell to Bramley & Maltby(Hellaby from 1920) were completed. The main portion of these was the Great Central & Midland jointly-owned Rotherham, Maltby & Laughton Railway which involved upgrading the Roundwood & Dalton Colliery line, including a new girder bridge over the Don at Thrybergh and connections to both the GC and Midland lines. The original bridge was retained to catch runaways from the severe gradient.

An Ivatt Class 2 2-6-2T and autocoach slip effortlessly across the viaduct carrying the Dearne Valley Railway over the River Don at Conisbrough on 8th September 1951. Standing 113ft tall, the viaduct was not only the most impressive railway structure on the line but arguably in the whole area. It survives, trackless, in 2009 as a monument to the achievements of another age. *N.E. Stead collection*

The H&B was also a partner in the Braithwell-Laughton section and the Thurcroft Colliery branch as it intended to build a line from Braithwell to Hickleton which did not materialise. A connecting spur between Laughton West on the RM&L and Laughton East on the South Yorkshire Joint was opened in January 1911, effectively rendering the Laughton West-Anston section redundant. But for a few workmen's trains, the RM&L was to remain freight only throughout its existence.

The Hull & Barnsley & Great Central Joint line running 21 miles northwards via Edlington and Sprotborough from Braithwell Junction to Gowdall, near Drax, where it joined the H&B's main line to Hull was finally opened in 1916 - seven years after being sanctioned by Parliament - having been delayed by legal wrangles, war and bad weather. Double track throughout in anticipation of heavy coal traffic, the line failed to fulfil its promoter's aspirations and spent much of its existence virtually dormant. The main line network reached its peak when between 1924 and 1929 the LNER opened lines from the SYJ at Firbeck Junction to serve Harworth and Firbeck collieries, both being originally promoted by the NER.

In the 1920s when the new deep mines and railways were in full production, C.B. Fawcett B.Litt., reader in Geography at Leeds University described the West and South Yorkshire coalfield in a booklet for the LNER thus: " It is a part of the largest coalfield in Britain, which extends eastwards as a "buried" field to the Humber and(on some estimates) the Wash......But the exposed part of the coalfield.....was the only part worked before the present(20th *sic*) century. Before the exploitation of the "buried" field there was no important export of coal from Yorkshire and its coal was mainly used in the development of many local manufacturing towns which have made it one of the most populous districts in this country."

Being a heavily industrialized area there were countless private sidings and industrial railways within steel works, colliery complexes and other plants, plus a small number of industrial lines connecting collieries with each other and the main lines. One of two notable industrial branches was the colliery railway which ran alongside the Greasborough Canal from exchange sidings with the GC Mexborough-Sheffield line at Rotherham Road to the NCC coke ovens and New Stubbin and Low Stubbin collieries, passing beneath the Midland line, to which it had a connection at Parkgate, on its way. The other, a colliery line opened in the 1920s, passed underneath the S&K to connect the massive coal preparation and coking complex at Manvers Main with Barnburgh Colliery two miles away. For about 13 years until 1909, the Greasborough Coal Company operated a totally isolated two-mile line from Greasborough Colliery to a landsale yard on Chapeltown Road, Rotherham, with a pair of Manning Wardle 0-4-0STs. The 1903 Ordnance Survey map shows a colliery line running via a rope-worked incline from Elsecar Goods, crossing over the Midland Barnsley-Sheffield line before passing its winding engine house and turning back to Lidgett Colliery at Wentworth & Hoyland Common. It also showed another incline descending from Hoyland Silkstone Colliery to the bank of a branch of the River Don Navigation opposite Elsecar Main Colliery. There was a staithe and coke ovens there but both incline tramways had gone by the time the 1930 map was published. Until 1954 Rotherham Main Colliery had its own line connecting it to the GC, part of it surviving until 1982 for use by British Steel.

The railways of this area cannot be mentioned without some reference to the waterways as the two were closely linked. The waterways were well established when the railways came on the scene, especially for moving bulk cargoes such as coal. In a ruthless bid to eliminate all competition, the early main line railways bought out the canals with the express intention of shutting them down but in the late 19th century, following Manchester's lead, local councils drew up proposals for a Sheffield Ship Canal and to this end they attempted to buy various local canals from the railways, notably the MS&L, for

On the South Yorkshire Joint at Firbeck West Junction (formerly Firbeck Junction 'A') on 31st March 1998. At 14.35 Type 5 No. 58015 heads a train of empty MGR hopper wagons towards Harworth Colliery. On the left, the SYJ continues to Doncaster and Kirk Sandall.
Since this picture was taken, Harworth Colliery has been mothballed, the Class 58s withdrawn and the familiar MGR hoppers mostly replaced by new high capacity bogie wagons.
Stephen Chapman

A 350hp 0-6-0 diesel shunter hired from BR, No. 08492, approaches the River Dearne crossing on the National Coal Board's Barnburgh Colliery line as it hauls a train of loaded NCB internal wagons to the Manvers Main coal preparation plant on 13th March 1989. *Adrian Booth*

conversion. As it turned out they did not have the money but in the 1980s funding from central government enabled the Sheffield & South Yorkshire Navigation incorporating the River Don, to be enlarged between Doncaster and Rotherham so that 700-tonne vessels could reach Mexborough and 400-tonne barges could reach Rotherham. Alas, it is mainly heavy lorries which carry most of the freight nowadays to the cost of canals and railways alike.

Passenger services

The first passenger trains through the area covered by this book were those along the North Midland Railway between Leeds, York, Derby, Birmingham and London(originally Euston) serving Rotherham's Masborough station as they would do for the next 146 years, as well as those between Rotherham Westgate and Sheffield (Wicker before Midland station was opened) which included through carriages between Sheffield and London via Masborough, a journey taking over nine hours. This sounds like forever nowadays but at that time was as good as reaching London in an instant.

From 1849, the Midland also ran a Sheffield Wicker-Doncaster service, using the NMR line to Swinton and the newly-opened South Yorkshire Railway through Mexborough and Conisbrough. In 1850, following full completion of the SYR between Mexborough and Barnsley, the Great Northern ran a Doncaster-Barnsley service which it reduced to just one train each way after only three years. For some reason, the Barnsley-Doncaster route was never blessed with an over-lavish passenger service despite the fact that it connected one of South Yorkshire's

principal towns with the East Coast main line. Nevertheless, upon completion of its Barnsley-Penistone line, the Manchester, Sheffield & Lincolnshire began a Penistone-Barnsley-Doncaster service in 1859 that was to last a hundred years.

From 1854 the SY ran a Doncaster-Sheffield Wicker service via Wath, Wombwell, Chapeltown and Wincobank, missing Rotherham by miles by using the SRBWH&G line which ultimately became the Great Central's Barnsley-Sheffield route. When the Mexborough-Rotherham-Sheffield route was opened in 1871, a new Doncaster-Sheffield Victoria via Rotherham service was introduced.

When the main line south from Sheffield to Chesterfield opened in 1870 it paved the way for some significant changes. Main line services to London, the Midlands and South West were rerouted via Sheffield, the original route between Masborough and Chesterfield via Treeton and Barrow Hill gaining the "Old Road" epithet by which many still know it today. A Sheffield-Chesterfield passenger service still ran this way, via the Holmes-Masborough South curve and serving Holmes and Treeton stations. It comprised five trains from Chesterfield and three from Sheffield in 1922. Some expresses still ran that way too, such as the 9.25am Glasgow-Bristol which left Masborough at 3.43pm and then ran non-stop to Derby. The local service lasted until 1954 while Treeton station closed in 1951. Since then, while remaining a busy trunk freight route, the Old Road has carried only passenger trains not required to call at Sheffield, notably summer Saturday holiday expresses, excursions and diverted trains. The Rotherham Westgate-Sheffield service was extended through to Manchester Central in 1894 when the Hope Valley line through the Peak District from Dore

& Totley was opened.

Completion of the S&K in 1879 brought a new passenger main line onto the scene and provided a more direct route for York-Sheffield trains. Following completion of the MS&L's London extension in 1899 long-distance expresses were soon introduced between the North East, York and the South Coast, South Wales and even Harwich via Rotherham Central (Rotherham & Masborough until 1950) and Sheffield Victoria. For this purpose, the Dearne Junction-Mexborough West Junction and Mexborough No.3 to No.1(west-south) curves began carrying passenger trains in 1899.

Some of the new lines opened in the 20th century to cash in on the output from the big deep coal mines of the concealed coalfield carried passenger services though generally they did not last long. A service ran along the H&B between Wath, Hickleton and Kirk Smeaton(on the H&B main line) until 1929. The L&Y introduced a Wakefield Kirkgate-Edlington service along the Dearne Valley line in 1912. It was operated by steam railmotors(formed of a conjoined 0-4-0 tank locomotive and driving carriage) serving what had to be the most basic stations ever to be found anywhere - each one consisting of a ground level sleeper platform and a lamp. They didn't even have any kind of shelter until old carriage bodies were eventually utilised. During the second world war the railmotors(or rather the locomotive portion) were replaced by a conventional push-pull operation using an ex-L&Y 2-4-2 "Radial" tank and the railmotor coach with the addition of a bogie at the end where it was previously fixed to its locomotive. Finally, the Radials were replaced by Ivatt Class 2 2-6-2Ts for the last years that the service operated.

One other passenger service through the area was that which from 1910 ran over the South Yorkshire Joint between Shireoaks and Doncaster, calling at Anston, Dinnington & Laughton, Maltby, and Tickhill & Wadworth stations. Consisting of just four trains each way(as well as Doncaster-Maltby workmen's trains,) it was operated jointly by the GC and the GNR. It led a chequered existence and after being reduced in 1911 became Saturday Only from 1917, presumably as a wartime expediency, and then reinstated as a(further reduced) Worksop-Doncaster service in 1920. It ceased again with the 1926 General Strike but was again reinstated in 1927 after legal threats from landowner Lord Scarborough with whom the railway had a binding agreement to provide Maltby with a passenger service. In 1929, however, it was reduced to one Worksop-Maltby train each way, the minimum required to fulfil the legal obligation to Lord Scarborough. Following assurances over parcels traffic with his Lordship, the service was withdrawn for the final time on 2nd December 1929.The stations were retained for use by occasional excursions up to the early 1960s.

During the 1950s and 60s, the era with which we are mainly concerned, the Midland line through Rotherham Masborough carried a mixture of long-distance expresses, including overnight sleeper trains, and local Leeds-Sheffield and York-Sheffield trains. The prestige trains - and easily through the whole area, for the route through Masborough was Britain's third Anglo-Scottish main line - were the London-Glasgow "Thames-Clyde Express," conveying a restaurant car and

usually in the hands of a Jubilee 4-6-0 until the BR/Sulzer Type 4 "Peak" diesels made their faltering entrance. In summer 1957 the Thames-Clyde left St. Pancras at 10.15am and Glasgow St. Enoch at 9.20am, passing Masborough around 1.40pm northbound and 3.20pm southbound. Alongside the Thames-Clyde were the 9.15am St. Pancras-Edinburgh and 10.5am Edinburgh-St. Pancras refreshment car expresses, at that time unnamed but christened "The Waverley" in 1957. The northbound train passed Masborough at approximately 12.45pm while the southbound train called there at 4.18pm. Besides these was the 6.40am Birmingham to Leeds and Bradford which on Saturdays conveyed through carriages from Derby to Glasgow that were attached to the 10.35 from Leeds.

A third named refreshment car express through Masborough in the summer was one which provided - for those who could afford it - an escape from the grimy, hard-working West Riding to altogether more delightful and doubtless sunnier climes. It was "The Devonian" - the 9.50am(9.5am on Saturdays) Bradford Forster Square to Paignton, and for the sombre return home, the 9.15am Paignton(8.45am from Kingswear on Saturdays) to Bradford. It passed Masborough at around 11.15 on the southbound run(around 40 minutes earlier on Saturdays when it went via the Old Road,) and called there at 5.21pm(5.16 on Sats) on the northbound run.

On weekdays there were four other St. Pancras to Leeds and Bradford expresses and five from Bradford and Leeds to St. Pancras; three Bradford/Leeds to Bristol trains, one from Bristol, and the 7pm Sheffield Midland to Heysham boat train.

Overnight sleeper trains in summer 1957 consisted of the 9pm St. Pancras-Edinburgh, the 9.15pm St. Pancras-Glasgow, the 11.50pm St. Pancras-Leeds, the 9.5pm Glasgow-St. Pancras and the 9.45pm Edinburgh-St. Pancras, plus Friday night reliefs, all of which slid through Masborough in the wee small hours except the 9.15pm and 11.50 pm from St. Pancras which called there, the former at around 2am and the latter at 5.27am.

Local services, which also followed the North Midland route via Wath North and Cudworth, included seven Leeds-Sheffield Midland trains each way, among them a highly nocturnal 2.10 am from Sheffield.There were also two Nottingham-Leeds trains, a 6.5pm Bradford Forster Square-Derby and a 3am Leeds-Sheffield which conveyed through carriages to Derby. In total, the number of Leeds-Sheffield express and local trains passing through Masborough every 24 hours on normal weekdays amounted to around 23 each way.

In summer 1922 Rotherham Westgate boasted an impressive service with 16 weekday departures to Sheffield and 15 trains coming in. The first departure of the day was at 5.35am and the last at 9.32pm. Four trains went to Manchester Central via the Hope Valley while the 5.35 went to Edale and the 9.32 to Hope. The 8am departure was an express running non-stop to Sheffield where it departed at 8.12 for Manchester. All other trains ran all stations to Sheffield. There was no Sunday service.

In addition to Leeds line trains were those to and from York via the S&K which, on Mondays to Fridays in summer 1957 amounted to 10 each way plus a small number of extras on odd days. Apart from four York to Sheffield Midland stopping trains and three the other way, all other trains consisted of long-

Dead on time and complete with horse box behind the engine, the northbound Waverley coasts through Rotherham Masborough at 12.42pm on 1st October 1960 with Jubilee 4-6-0 No. 45619 *Nigeria* **in charge. One of the premier trains on the Midland main line through Masborough, this St. Pancras-Edinburgh express was once named The Thames-Forth Express, becoming The Waverley in 1957 after a period of anonymity.** *Robert Anderson*

distance North East-South West services, known nowadays as Cross-Country. They comprised two Newcastle-Bristol trains each way, a Newcastle-Cardiff and a Newcastle-Birmingham each way, three Bristol to York trains and two from York to-Bristol, and one from Worcester to York. The overnight 7.20pm Bristol-Newcastle and 7.5pm Newcastle-Bristol were mail trains. The 3.57pm Newcastle-Birmingham continued to Penzance on Fridays when it also conveyed through carriages for Newquay. Additional trains consisted of the 8.35am Bristol-York which ran from 22nd July to 30th August, the Fridays Only 2.15pm York-Birmingham and 9.5pm Newcastle-Paignton. With national service at its height, a number of troop trains to and from Catterick Camp ran through the area. On Sunday nights in 1955 they were the 8.15pm from Gloucester and 7.35pm from Bristol which were advertised public services as far as Darlington; the unadvertised Friday 3.50pm Richmond-Birmingham, and the Saturday 12.20pm Catterick-Birmingham, advertised from Darlington.

Also using the Midland line through Masborough was a limited service between Sheffield Midland and Hull via the Swinton-Mexborough curve. In summer 1957, it consisted of the 3.10pm, and 5.45pm high summer Fridays only from Sheffield and the 9.12am, and 10.10pm Fridays Only from Hull. The 5.45 from Sheffield combined with the 5.20pm Sheffield Victoria-Hull at Doncaster while the 10.10pm from Hull conveyed through carriages to Paignton in high summer.

Three regularly timetabled mid-week York trains each way via the S&K in summer 1957 took the GC line via the Dearne Junction-Mexborough West curve, Rotherham Central and Sheffield Victoria. They included the 10.23 York to Bournemouth calling Rotherham Central at 11.33(and Bolton-

on-Dearne on Fridays at 11.15) and 11.16am Bournemouth-York(Rotherham Central at 6.25pm and Bolton-on-Dearne on Fridays at 6.43) - noted for their green Southern Region carriages which appeared on alternate days. Others were the 12.20pm York-Banbury(to Swansea on Fridays) and 12.58pm Banbury-York(8.15am Swansea-Newcastle on Fridays) and the overnight 10.22pm York-Swindon and 9.40pm Swindon-York, all of which passed through Rotherham Central without stopping. The Swindon trains called at Swinton Central when required to set down or pick up train crews. One additional summer season train was the 8.17am Sheffield Victoria-Scarborough which left Rotherham Central at 8.30 and ran from 15th July to 30th August.

The bulk of the GC line service was provided by Hull-Doncaster-Sheffield trains and top of the list were the Hull-Liverpool Central refreshment car expresses which travelled via Sheffield Victoria and the Woodhead line. Calling also at Mexborough and Rotherham Central they left Hull at 9.24am and 4.18pm and Liverpool at 9.30am and 4.30pm in summer 1957. The line also saw another three trains from Sheffield Victoria to Hull and two from Hull to Sheffield Victoria on weekdays. A handful of local trains ran between Sheffield Victoria and Doncaster and in winter 1956/57 these included the 1.48am Leeds-Doncaster-Sheffield class A passenger and parcels and the 4.20am Sheffield-Doncaster-Leeds class A, and the 2.45 and 8.50pm Sheffield-Doncaster-York, both class B. One other main line train was the often heavily loaded 6.30pm York-Swindon which started from Scarborough in high summer and was booked to stop at Rotherham Central to attach an assisting engine when required for the steeply graded stretch to Sheffield. There was also a 4.52am Mondays Excepted

In this view by our anonymous contributor to whom we are always most grateful, a BR/Sulzer 'Peak' Type 4 approaches Holmes Junction with the Saturdays Only 09.40 Bradford Forster Square to Paignton in July 1966. The Alma iron works was on the right.

Doncaster-Sheffield Victoria parcels. As the engine then worked back with the 8am Sheffield-Doncaster stopper it had to run light from Doncaster shed on Mondays.

Services between Mexborough and Doncaster were augmented by the few Penistone-Barnsley-Doncaster trains. In the winter 1956/57 working timetable these comprised five trains each way on weekdays(including the 6.5am Mexborough-Penistone) plus the 12.35am non-stop Mexborough-Penistone unadvertised workmen's train. The only Sunday trains were the workmen's train and the 2.30am Penistone-Doncaster news and passenger(with news vans detached from the 1.25am Manchester-Cleethorpes) which called at Wath Central when required. A Manchester-Scarborough train each way running via Penistone and Barnsley used the Wath-Dearne Junction spur on summer Saturdays during the 1950s and early 1960s. In summer 1960 these trains left Manchester London Road at 9.55am, calling at Bolton-on-Dearne at 11.34, and Scarborough at 10am and passing Wath Junction at 1pm. The LNER ran Manchester-Scarborough excursions via the spur before the second world war.

Terminating as it did just short of Doncaster, the Dearne Valley service was strictly local, linking the mining communities along its route with Wakefield. Five weekday trains ran each way in summer 1939, one afternoon train each way between Wakefield and Goldthorpe & Thurnscoe only. These trains left Wakefield Kirkgate at 8.10 and 10.25am, 1.5, 3.50 and 5.45pm, and Edlington at at 9.18, and 11.33 am, 2.13 and 6.50pm, and Goldthorpe & Thurnscoe at 4.40pm(the return working of the 3.50 from Wakefield.) Two extra trains ran each way between Wakefield and Goldthorpe & Thurnscoe on Saturday evenings.

For around 12 weeks in the summer, Saturdays would see thousands of holidaymakers on the move as they began and

ended their summer holidays on that one day of the week. Those few days of the year were hectic times for the railways almost as much in industrial South Yorkshire as in the holiday resorts themselves. Summer Saturdays in summer 1957 brought more than 40 extra trains originating and terminating in Sheffield and Rotherham or passing through. A number ran via the Old Road, avoiding Sheffield. On the long-distance routes they included Newcastle-Paignton, Newquay-Newcastle and Newquay-York trains, the 8.25am Hull-Birmingham, the 8.31pm Friday(1955 time) Newcastle-Paington which was an unadvertised relief, the 9.42pm(1955) Newcastle-Bournemouth, the 9am Glasgow-St. Pancras, the 9.50am Edinburgh-Sheffield, and the 9.20am St. Pancras-Glasgow which made no passenger stops between Sheffield and Carlisle, passing through Masborough at about 1.28pm Also on the Midland line were the 6.10am Nottingham-Craigendoran and 12.12pm return(1955 times) which were unadvertised specials run on behalf of the Creative Tourist Agents Conference. Summer nights on the GC saw the so-called "Starlight Specials" which were also not advertised in the public timetable. In 1955 they were the Friday 9.45pm and 10.5pm(when required) Marylebone-Edinburgh and 9.23pm(when required) and 9.40pm Edinburgh-Marylebone. They all avoided Sheffield Victoria, as did the summer Saturdays 11.16am Bournemouth-Newcastle by taking the Darnall West curve onto the Mexborough line.

Saturday trains to/from the Yorkshire coast included trains from Gloucester Eastgate and Sheffield Victoria to Filey Holiday Camp, between Leicester - Central and London Road - and Scarborough, Derby and Scarborough, and King's Norton and Scarborough. For local holidaymakers there were Sheffield Midland-Scarborough and Sheffield Victoria-Bridlington trains plus the 7.45am Rotherham Central-Bridlington and 1.25pm return.

Trains to the Lancashire coast in summer 1957 comprised the 6.50am Sheffield and 7.5am Rotherham Masborough to Blackpool(two separate trains) and the 2.20pm return to Sheffield which called all stations from Cudworth to Masborough to set down only; the 7.50am Sheffield-Morecambe and 11.30am return; and the 5.50am Nottingham-Morecambe and 1.50pm return which called at Swinton Town to set down only before passing non-stop through Masborough and continuing via the Old Road.

Nationalisation and the formation of British Railways in 1948(renamed British Rail from 1965) brought some fairly instant economies and three passenger services were axed before the 1960s Beeching Plan was ever heard of. First to go was the Dearne Valley service, withdrawn on 10th September 1951. On 4th October 1952 the last passenger trains used Rotherham Westgate station and in 1954 the Old Road lost its local service. The 1950s ended with the closure of Wath Central and Wombwell Central stations upon withdrawal of the Doncaster-Barnsley-Penistone service on 29th June 1959, leaving just the overnight newspaper train which continued until 1970 when it ceased carrying passengers until after Doncaster. During the 1960s the loss of local trains between Mexborough and Doncaster was compensated by extension of some Cleethorpes-Doncaster trains to and from Sheffield. Although the late 1950s saw the replacement steam with diesel multiple units on most local services with resulting economies, it was too late for those already axed.

With these closures over, the 1960s did not bring the same cataclysmic cuts as in many other, less fortunate areas, though one notable cut was the withdrawal of the Hull-Liverpool Central through trains at the start of the winter 1962 timetable.

A major scheme to modernise the Sheffield area, which included the concentration of all passenger services on Sheffield Midland did however bring far reaching changes. New connections laid between the Midland and GC lines where they passed close to each other at Aldwarke - mainly to facilitate the movement of freight trains to and from the new Tinsley marshalling yard - meant that Doncaster-Mexborough-Sheffield Victoria trains could be switched to Masborough and Midland stations, and the GC line between Aldwarke and Woodburn Junction(Sheffield) closed to passengers. After the Doncaster trains were switched to Masborough on 4th October 1965 the only passenger trains passing through Rotherham Central were the York-Bournemouth, Bournemouth-York and York-Swindon which still had to call at Sheffield Victoria in order to reach the GC main line to the south - but that only until 5th September 1966 when the GC main line ceased to be a through route, and when Rotherham Central closed.

On 1st January 1968 the Sheffield-Leeds local service via Cudworth was withdrawn leaving Rotherham with no stopping trains to Leeds; Wath North, Swinton Town(used the following summer as an unstaffed halt for a handful of summer Saturday trains), Kilnhurst West and Parkgate & Rawmarsh stations were all closed to passengers(Darfield having closed in 1963,) and expresses switched to the S&K via Moorthorpe. Two years later, although only indirectly affecting the area in this book, came the axing of the Sheffield Victoria-Manchester Piccadilly electric service via Penistone and the complete closure of Victoria station. Thus the Woodhead line was rendered freight only between Penistone and Hadfield(the limit of suburban services from Manchester,) although it was still used for planned and emergency passenger train diversions for some years after. The North Midland line through Cudworth did not immediately become entirely freight only. Passenger services still shown in the

One of the original Midland Railway Compound 4-4-0s, No. 41021 of Sheffield Millhouses, heads southbound past Masborough Sorting Sidings with late 1940s summer excursion No.279. As was often the case with summer Saturday extras, the train was composed of non-corridor stock and therefore no access to toilets which could make it seem a long journey, especially for passengers with children. *Tom Greaves*

1968/69 working timetable as travelling that way included the 00.05 St. Pancras-Leeds, the 06.40 Birmingham-Leeds(Glasgow on summer Saturdays,) the 09.20 summer Saturday St. Pancras-Glasgow, 02.00 Sheffield Midland-Leeds class 1 passenger and 03.00 Leeds-Derby mail, the 07.40 Sheffield-Leeds(to Morecambe on summer Saturdays) and 10.36 Sheffield-Leeds class 2 passenger, the 19.22 Leeds-Derby passenger, the 21.40 Leeds-Sheffield mail, the 22.15 Leeds-St. Pancras, an overnight Stirling-Newhaven Motorail in each direction and several long-distance parcels trains. By the start of the 1969/70 timetable, however, all had been rerouted via Moorthorpe, while it would doubtless please Hudson's ghost to see that the one remaining London-Scotland sleeper service had begun running to and from Euston instead of St. Pancras, but still via the North Midland through Rotherham.

By the start of the 1970s, the remaining passenger services through the area consisted of North East-South West expresses and a few St. Pancras trains via Moorthorpe, York-Sheffield local trains and the Sheffield-Doncaster service which had been improved with 18 trains each weekday from Sheffield and 16 to Sheffield in the May 1970-May 1971 timetable. The Doncaster-Sheffield service by then was a mixture of Doncaster, Hull and Cleethorpes-Sheffield diesel multiple units. Notable exceptions were the 18.40(19.02 on Saturdays) York-Sheffield DMU(a loco-hauled train from Scarborough on certain dates in the summer) and 21.25 return which ran via Doncaster, the 09.54 Cleethorpes-Sheffield which was loco-hauled on summer Saturdays, and the 19.55 Bristol-Newcastle.

By 1978 several trains a day were running between Hull or Cleethorpes and Manchester Piccadilly, providing Rotherham with eight through trains a day to the other side of the Pennines.

The following year, Trans-Pennine Class 124 and former Western Region Class 123 Inter-City diesel units were assigned to the service. In the 1980s, as the condition of these elderly units became a matter of concern, some LIverpool-Sheffield trains were made loco-hauled and one ran each way between Cleethorpes and Liverpool via Doncaster, calling at Conisbrough, Mexborough and Rotherham.

The whole situation regarding the North Midland line was reversed in May 1973 when an agreement between BR and the National Coal Board over the extent of coal mining and the resulting subsidence - and due to worsening subsidence on the S&K - saw almost all North East-South West and Midland line expresses - including those which had always travelled via the S&K - rerouted via Cudworth. A memorable late 1970s and early 1980s express was the Edinburgh-Plymouth which could be powered from York by a Class 50 returning to the Western Region after overhaul at Doncaster. The York-Sheffield local service was increased to compensate for the loss of expresses previously serving Bolton-on-Dearne and Pontefract.

Electrification of the West Coast main line to Scotland in 1974 and the introduction of 125mph High Speed Trains on the East Coast main line in 1978 saw the Midland route cease to be an Anglo-Scottish main line of any real importance. The St. Pancras-Glasgow and Edinburgh expresses, including the famous Thames-Clyde and the sleeper service had been replaced by just three Nottingham-Carlisle/Glasgow trains each way. In summer 1978 these were the 07.15, 10.25 from Nottingham and 16.05(15.51 on Saturdays) Nottingham-Carlisle, and the 09.35 from Carlisle and 11.50 and 16.10 from Glasgow.

Class 5 4-6-0 No. 44756, fitted with Caprotti valve gear, Timken roller bearings and double chimney, restarts the 4.15pm Leeds to Sheffield Midland stopping train from Rotherham Masborough at 5.50pm on 3rd April 1961. *Robert Anderson*

Another former Western Region class 123 diesel multiple unit arrives for work on the Hull-Sheffield-Liverpool service. It is seen being towed towards Wath Yard on 3rd December 1980 by EM1 Bo-Bo electrics Nos. 76011 and 76029. *Adrian Booth*

Leeds-St. Pancras expresses were down to just one each way.

The 1968 Transport Act helped secure the future of surviving passenger services by providing Grant Aid for unrenumerative services. In 1969-1971, the Sheffield Doncaster service was awarded £137,000 a year, the Sheffield-York service £83,000 in 1969 and 1970 and Leeds-Rotherham-Sheffield, a service by then provided mainly by Inter-City trains, £107000 for 1969. In the 1970s the newly-formed South Yorkshire Passenger Transport Executive was formed to co-ordinate, safeguard and improve public transport. In the early years the PTE was notably bus-orientated but did subsidise some local rail services including a new peak hour Rotherham-Sheffield shuttle.

The 1980s saw some truly radical alterations which shaped the services operating in 2009, including the final elimination of Anglo-Scottish trains on the Midland line via Rotherham and Leeds. The Nottingham-Glasgow/Carlisle services were axed in the early 1980s as the Settle & Carlisle line was prepared for closure(which thankfully did not happen,) a Nottingham-Leeds service of five trains each way on weekdays being introduced in May 1986.

A new management structure on BR, specifically the formation of the InterCity business sector, brought new thinking. The opening of the East Coast main line Selby diversion between Doncaster and York in 1983 provided new opportunities while a major earth slip north of Cudworth, long-distance coach competition and recession all influenced the decision to drop plans for a multi-million pound 115mph upgrade of the Wath Road-Normanton portion of the North Midland line to maximise the speed potential of recently-introduced High Speed

Trains. Instead, many Cross-Country services, as the North East-South West route had been rebranded, were rerouted via Doncaster while most Leeds trains reverted to the S&K via Moorthorpe. Two summer dated trains, the Friday 22.39 Bradford-Paignton and the Saturday 07.39 Leicester-Scarborough became the last passenger trains to use the Cudworth route until they too were rerouted after summer 1986.

By this time, the PTE had become much more rail-minded and was pumping investment into passenger facilities and services which included the opening of a new single track spur from Holmes Junction to the GC line through Rotherham thus enabling services to run directly between Sheffield Midland and a new Rotherham Central station. The Holmes Chord and the new station opened on 11th May 1987 when all Sheffield-Doncaster trains and the Leeds-Nottingham service were switched to the new route. In July, BR proposed the closure of Masborough station with effect from 5th October. In the event there were a number of objections and the closure did not take effect until 16th May 1988 when York-Sheffield trains were rerouted via Central, a new Sheffield-Rotherham-Leeds via Moorthorpe service introduced, and new stations opened on the S&K at Goldthorpe and Thurnscoe. Between May 1987 and May 1988, six Sheffield-York and seven York-Sheffield trains were the only ones still to call at Masborough along with the 1987 summer Saturday 09.48 Moorthorpe-Blackpool and 14.22 return and the 07.52 Leicester-Scarborough and 11.48 return InterCity. Other InterCity services, including the still extant Devonian, passed through Masborough without stopping and the only other passenger trains to call there, for a time, were football specials because of its proximity to Rotherham United's Millmoor ground. In 1990 a new station was opened at Swinton on the Midland line, served by Sheffield-Doncaster trains rerouted via the reinstated Swinton curve, as well as Sheffield-York and Leeds services. InterCity trains via Doncaster were also rerouted round the curve, the Aldwarke-Mexborough section of the GC line becoming freight only.

Increasing car ownership and overseas package holidays coupled with BR economies including a massive cull of spare coaching stock saw a big reduction in summer Saturday specials to the coast during the late 1960s which continued during the 1970s and 1980s until such trains barely exist in 2009.

By summer 1978 the only booked summer Saturday train on the Doncaster line apart from a couple of additional Sheffield-Cleethorpes and Scarborough trains was the 08.37 Leicester-Scarborough which came via the Old Road. The few remaining summer Saturday trains via the S&K to York included the 07.05 from Wellingborough, 09.07 from Birmingham and the 12.40 Scarborough-Leicester besides a handful of Sheffield-Scarborough/Bridlington trains. There were still, however, a good many summer Saturday trains between the North East, Leeds and the West Country and remained so until services were privatised in the 1990s. In 2004 Virgin Trains was forced to reintroduce a loco-hauled summer Saturday Paignton-Newcastle train because its new Voyager diesel units proved woefully inadequate for all the extra passengers and their luggage. Hauled by Class 67 locomotives hired from freight operator EWS they passed non-stop through the closed Masborough station though one occasionally ran via Central for drivers' route knowledge purposes. The Leicester-Scarborough is one summer Saturday survivor, still running in 2008 as the St. Pancras-Scarborough operated by a Midland Main Line "Meridian" Class 222 diesel unit.

In 2009 Rotherham is served by hourly Leeds-Moorthorpe-Sheffield trains, hourly Hull-Sheffield trains, hourly Lincoln-Sheffield-Doncaster-Scunthorpe or Adwick trains, and a very sparse York-Sheffield service. CrossCountry expresses and Cleethorpes-Manchester Airport TransPennine Express services pass non-stop through the bare and unused Masborough platforms.

Freight traffic

Being one of Britain's most heavily industrialized areas, this neck of the woods saw very intense freight traffic until comparatively recently. It can be said that freight flows were mainly of four different types: the many local trips which connected various yards, collieries, steel plants, works sidings and depots; coal workings in and out of Wath marshalling yard including those across the Pennines via the Worsborough branch and the Woodhead line; medium distance freights both originating and terminating in the area and passing through, and long-distance express freights passing through. Back in the 1950s and early 1960s, the vast majority were class 8 loose-coupled trains fitted with no continuous brake. As the 1960s passed, more trains became fitted with vacuum brake on most or all wagons and, from the 1970s onwards with air brakes.

Prior to the opening of Tinsley marshalling yard in 1965,

A Derby Works Class 108 DMU forming a Sheffield-York service calls at the new 3-platform Swinton station as crowds gather for the official opening ceremony on 14th May 1990. *Stephen Chapman*

Masborough Sorting Sidings was the focal point for many Midland line freight workings with other yards at Roundwood, Parkgate, Woodhouse Mill and in the Sheffield area, while on the GC lines there were yards at Mexborough, Ickles, Rotherham Road, Thrybergh and Barnsley Junction(Penistone) as well as the marshalling yard at Wath.

The summer 1963 freight working timetable gives a good indication of the type and quantity of freight workings in the area during the Railway Memories era.

Most Midland line freight ran via the Old Road and Masborough Sorting Sidings, situated between Masborough station and Canklow. Then, as today, only Hope Valley traffic and traffic for Sheffield went via the Sheffield line. In 1963 more than 230 (over 110 northbound and over 120 southbound) freights were booked to run over the Midland line in the Rotherham area every 24 hours, not counting numerous light engine or engine and brake van movements - that's an average of a train every six minutes! Trips workings alone are too numerous to detail and involve just about every permutation of origins and destinations one can think of. These are shown below.

Masborough Sorting Sidings-Wincobank Sidings & v.v.*
Masborough Sorting Sidings-Roundwood Sidings & v.v.,
Masborough Sorting Sidings-Parkgate & v.v.
Masborough Sorting Sidings-Masborough Station Yard & v.v.
Masborough Sorting Sidings-Mexborough & v.v.
Masborough Sorting Sidings-Harrison & Camm Ltd.
Carlton Sidings(Cudworth)- Masborough Sorting Sidings
Kilnhurst West-Masborough Sorting Sidings
Parkgate & Rawmarsh-Masborough Sorting Sidings
Barnsley Top Yard-Masborough Sorting Sidings
Roundwood Sidings-Parkgate & Rawmarsh
Roundwood Sidings-Firth's Sidings(Sheffield)
Roundwood Sidings-Carlton Sidings & v.v.
Roundwood Sidings-Parkgate Junction
Roundwood Sidings-Kilnhurst West
Roundwood Sidings-Wicker, Brightside and Attercliffe.
Wath Yard-Roundwood Sidings
Wincobank-Roundwood Sidings & v.v.
Wincobank-Parkgate & Rawmarsh
Woodhouse Mill-Parkgate & Rawmarsh
Woodhouse Mill-Roundwood Sidings
Woodhouse Mill-Firth's Sidings*
Woodhouse Mill-Sheffield Upwell Street.*
Woodhouse Mill-Wincobank Sidings*
Chesterfield Midland-Sheffield Wicker*
Sheffield Wicker/Grimesthorpe Engine Shed Sidings-
              Masborough Sorting Sidings*
Catcliffe-West Tinsley*
Sheffield Cardigan Sidings-Firth Brown's Canklow tip*
* via Masborough South-Holmes curve

A sample trip duty is 8T38 which worked as follows:

4.5am MX	Masborough Sorting Sidings-Mexborough Top Yard
5.55am	Mexborough Top Yard-Wincobank Sidings
8.18am	Wincobank Sidings-Parkgate & Rawmarsh(9T38)
10.10am	Parkgate & Rawmarsh-Roundwood Sidings
11.10am	Roundwood Sidings-Parkgate & Rawmarsh
12.10pm	Parkgate & Rawmarsh-Masborough Sorting Sidings

Besides these were trips directly serving Manvers Main, Hickleton, Frickley, Renishaw and Treeton collieries and Orgreave coke works. A daily trip also fed Carr House gas works, Parkgate, with coal from Frickley Colliery.

Masborough Sorting Sidings dealt with over 150 trains every 24 hours. Most were local trips but medium or longer distance trains originating there went to Toton, Washwood Heath, Stanton Gate, Norton Junction, York, Stourton, Glasgow(4S56 at 8.30pm - an Assured Arrival service,) Immingham, Chaddesden(Derby,) Barrow Hill and Cudworth. Arrivals came from Norton Junction, Seymour Junction, London Somers Town(a class 4 fully fitted), Stourton, and Normanton.

Long-distance, mainly class 8, freights passing through the area - some booked to call at Masborough Sorting Sidings - included trains from Birmingham(Lawley Street,) Wincobank Sidings, Woodhouse Mill and Toton to Normanton, Chaddesden to Hunslet and Normanton and vice versa; Normanton to Washwood Heath and Roundwood Sidings; Water Orton to Leeds Hunslet; Tees Yard to Chaddesden; York to Toton, Toton to Tees Yard, Toton to Hunslet; Roundwood Sidings, Manvers Main and Cudworth to Toton; Barrow Hill and Shirebrook to Carlton Sidings; Stourton to Roundwood Sidings and Sheffield Wicker; Avenue Sidings(Clay Cross) to Roundwood Sidings and Stourton; Gowhole to Manvers Main; and Carnforth to Roundwood Sidings and Firth's Sidings. Some GC line freights such as the 10.20am York-Annesley and 3.40pm Woodford Halse-Tees were routed via Masborough to interchange with Midland line traffic.

A number of workings used the Swinton curve to reach the GC lines at Mexborough; they included coke and iron ore trains between the East Midlands and Scunthorpe. Other such trains were a Parkgate-Hull empties, coal empties from Corby to Cadeby Colliery, a Thorne Colliery-Roundwood coal train, Woodhouse Mill-Frodingham and Normanby Park-Water Orton freights, the 10.25pm Doncaster-Roundwood Assured Arrival service, plus Roundwood and Masborough-Mexborough trips. Iron ore trains from the East Midlands, often powered until the 1950s by the mighty LMS Garratts but by this time more likely to be a Wellingborough-based Crosti-boilered 9F 2-10-0, were a notable feature of freight operations. The majority also took the Swinton curve en-route to the big iron works at Scunthorpe and Frodingham while others travelled north along the S&K to the North East. Trains from Storefield booked to go to either Normanby Park or West Hartlepool were class 4 fully braked.

Several workings to and from Wath Yard also used the Swinton curve with a reversal at Mexborough but others travelled via Dearne Junction where they reversed by having a pilot engine attached to the rear which then hauled the train and its engine down to Wath. Similarly, trains in the opposite direction were drawn by the pilot(attached at Moor Road) with the train engine on the rear up to Dearne Junction from where the train engine worked forward.

Amidst all these trips and slow loose-coupled trains, came a host of fully-braked long-distance express freights. Many were fast overnight-delivery services and the small hours were their domain. Of the highest status were trains 3S60 and 3M29, the

A typical class 8 through freight hauled by 4F 0-6-0 No. 44097 comes off the "Old Road' and approaches Masborough station at 10am on 1st October 1960. Masborough goods depot is visible through the bridge on the left. *Robert Anderson*

7.23pm Hendon to Gushetfaulds and 7.50 Gushetfaulds-Hendon "Condor," passing through Masborough at 11.10pm and 1.55am respectively. Initially powered by pairs of the ill-starred Metrovick Co-Bo diesels, this all-container train introduced in 1959 was a pioneer in inter-modal transport. It made its last run on 26th October 1967 when it was replaced by a new Freightliner service.The only other train of equal status to the Condor was the 9.15pm 3M15 York to Birmingham fish which ran via Sheffield.

Next in the pecking order were the class 4 express freights, fitted with continuous brake on at least 90 per cent of wagons. These included the largely daytime Birmingham-Carlisle freights(from Water Orton on the outward and to Washwood Heath on the return,) worked by Saltley engines(usually 9F 2-10-0s) and men throughout. There were also class 4 trains from Lawley Street and Water Orton to Hunslet, Whitacre to Hull (when required,) Willesden to Carlisle, Woodford Halse-York each way, Leicester-Carlisle, Nottingham to Carlisle, Leicester-York, Lawley Street-York, Bristol to York Dringhouses, Luton-Bonniebridge(when required,) Tyne Yard-Lawley Street, Glasgow to St. Pancras, Hurlford to Brent, York to Washwood Heath, Glasgow to Washwood Heath, Stourton to Wigston, Carlisle to Leicester, Greenhill-Wilshampstead(when required,) Carlisle-Stoke Gifford, Bradford-St. Pancras, Stourton-Wigston, Stourton-St. Pancras, Bradford-Westerleigh Junction, Bradford-Nottingham, Hull-Washwood Heath, Sheffield Wicker-St. Pancras, Stourton-Leicester, and the 7.50pm Bristol Severn Beach to Tees which ran when required.

Also running class 4 were the legendary beer trains from Burton-on-Trent and one can ponder at length just how much beer flowed through Masborough station each evening! Conveying their amber cargo were the 6.10pm Burton-York, the 8.2pm Burton-Carlisle and the 9.10pm Mondays Only Burton-Millerhill.

Of course, just across the way, another procession of freight trains pounded along the GC line through Rotherham. There were fewer than on the Midland, around 116 every 24 hours(63 southbound and 53 northbound,) not including light engine movements. Many workings emanated from Sheffield Bernard Road which was the main sorting yard for the GC lines in the area. A total of 17 trip duties plied their way along the Sheffield-Mexborough line between the various yards, steel works, collieries and private sidings. Below are their various origins and destinations:

Bernard Road-Ickles
Bernard Road-Rotherham Road
Wath Yard-Bernard Road
Broughton Lane-Rotherham Road
Broughton Lane-Ickles
Broughton Lane-Wath Yard
Neepsend-Wath Yard
Mexborough-Bernard Road
Mexborough Top Yard-Templeborough
Ickles-Wath Yard & v.v.
Ickles-Don Bridge East & v.v.

Ickles-Orgreave
Ecclesfield East-Ickles
Chapeltown Central-Ickles
Wath Yard-Greasborough Road
Greasborough Road-Ickles
Rotherham Central-Rotherham Road
Rotherham Central-Ickles
Meadow Hall-Ickles
Sheffield Engine Shed Sidings(Midland)-Ickles
Silverwood-Wath Yard

As with the Midland lines, ordinary through freights ran between an interminable variety of origins and destinations. The most common routes were Wath-Staveley Central, Wath-Ickles, Ickles-Frodingham, York-Staveley Central and York-Annesley. Trains also passed through on their way from Normanby Park, Frodingham, Ardsley, Stockton-on-Tees, Mexborough to Annesley and vice-versa; between Hull and Bernard Road; Woodford Halse and Frodingham; Bernard Road and York; Frodingham and Meadow Hall; Stainforth, Bernard Road and Deepcar; Neepsend, Broughton Lane and Wath; Renishaw and Manvers Main, and Wath and Renishaw. There were also trains from Wath yard and Denaby 'A' Colliery to Toton and Ickles to Barrow Hill, both Midland line destinations. Many through trains were booked to stop at Rotherham Road for anything up to 30 minutes. They also left Ickles Sidings for Worksop, Annesley, Wath and Mottram via Wath, and they arrived at Ickles from Bernard Road, Doncaster, and Annesley, and at Rotherham Road from Godley Junction, Seymour Junction and Ardsley.

Besides these was a class 4 fully-fitted iron ore train which arrived at Aldwarke Main Colliery Sidings(for the new Aldwarke

steel works) from High Dyke, near Grantham, at 9.17pm with an extra working on Saturdays arriving at 2.9pm. A class 8 ore train also came in from Crosby Mines, North Lincs., booked to arrive at 2.56pm. There were nowhere near as many fully braked express freights as on the Midland. Class 4 trains over the line in summer 1963 were the 3.32am MX 4N26 Woodford Halse-Hull; 6.35pm 4N23 Woodford Halse-York; 12.45pm 4N08 Barry Docks-Bradford Adolphus Street(when required;) 1.30am MX 4M26 Hull-Annesley; 2.30am MX 4E80 York Dringhouses-Sheffield Bridgehouses; 3.10am 4M21 York Dringhouses-Woodford Halse; 3.55am MX 4V24 York-Banbury; 12.25am MX 4V21 Tees Yard (5.10am MO Dringhouses)-Cardiff; and the 2.20am MX 4V23 Tees Yard(6.5am MO Dringhouses)-Bristol. Class 5 freights, with continuous brake on more than half the wagons, also passed through on their way between Bernard Road and Hull, Dewsnap and Hull, Woodford Halse and Ardsley and Doncaster Belmont and Bridgehouses.

There were something like 230 trains in and out or passing through Wath Yard every 24 hours on weekdays in summer 1963, not counting light engines and trains which ran only on one or two days a week. Most of the traffic was coal but there were other classes of freight too. Around 85 trains were outgoing at the west end, about half of which took the electrified lines via Worsborough, Penistone and Woodhead - an average of nearly one every half hour round the clock. A few went only as far as Barnsley Junction sidings at Penistone but most went to Mottram Yard, eleven miles short of Manchester. Here, incoming wagons from Yorkshire were sorted and remarshalled into trains for their final destinations in Lancashire, Cheshire and Merseyside. Just about the only westbound trains not destined for Mottram at that time were the 6.45pm MWFO Wath-

Class 37 diesels on freight duty at Aldwarke on 31st January 1968. No. D6810 has charge of the class 7 unfitted express freight bound for the Doncaster division while D6800 waits with a local trip. *Adrian Booth*

Ravenhead(St. Helens) and the 7.10pm Wath-Shotwick. The majority of westbound trains started from Wath and most were class 8. The exceptions were two Frodingham-Mottram class 8s, the 1.25pm 8M35 Tees Yard-Mottram, the 5.40pm 7M06 Kirk Sandall-Mottram, the 10.15pm 5M14 Hull to Mottram fitted, the 9.45pm 5M13 Ardsley-Mottram which combined with the 11.35pm 4E52 from York Dringhouses at Elsecar Junction, and the 9.17pm Cudworth-Mottram which reversed and changed locos for an electric at Wombwell Exchange. It is interesting to note that the working timetable designated the Wath-Barnsley Junction and Mottram trains as "electric" but not necessarily others travelling via Woodhead. Electrification did not entirely eliminate steam from the Worsborough branch, some local trips such as those serving Wentworth Silkstone Colliery remained steam until diesels took over. Also changing locos to an electric loco at Wath, between 9.45 and 10.5pm, was what could be termed the line's premier freight train - the 7.45pm 4M40 Hull to Guide Bridge fish. Coal trains departed for Elland Power Station, near Halifax, at 10.15pm and 1.30am.

There were approximately 85 booked incoming trains from the west, again about half coming down the bank from Penistone and the Woodhead line. Eastbound, the train pattern was quite different. Whereas most westbound trains ran from Wath to Mottram, eastbound trains came from a variety of origins and a good many did not terminate at Wath but continued to their their final destinations. Thirteen trains originated at Dewsnap Sidings, Guide Bridge, and most went forward to Doncaster, Ardsley, Frodingham, York, Tees Yard and Stainforth with one for Barnsley Main Colliery reversing and changing locos at Wombwell Exchange. Trains also came from Godley Junction, Northwich, Glazebrook, Bidston, Cornbrook,

Ashburys and Trafford Park. There were two class 4 fully fitted express freights: the 7.30pm 4N28 Huskisson(Liverpool)-York and the 9.45pm 4N25 Ancoates(Manchester)-Hull. Another working worthy of mention is the 9.5am Mondays and Wednesdays Only Mexborough motive power depot to Gorton Works locomotives for repair and the 5.50am ex-Gorton. Eastbound locomotive changes from electric to steam or diesel generally took place at Wath Exchange, at the east end of the yard, while westbound locomotive changes were mostly at Wombwell Main Junction. Wombwell Main could be accommodating up to six banking engines when the line was at its busiest

A total of 85 booked trains came and went at Wath's east end. Besides those already mentioned, they came from Hull, Frodingham, Doncaster, Grimsby West Marsh, Stainforth, Warmsworth Junction and Bullcroft Junction, and went to Doncaster, Kirk Sandall, Frodingham, Normanby Park and Goole. A daily return through freight, class 7 outward and class 8 return ran between Doncaster Belmont and Barnsley Top Yard. The 8.30am Wath Yard to Ickles and 7.25am Broughton Lane to Wath Yard class 8s were by 1963 the only trains to run the full length of the GC Barnsley-Sheffield route.

Local trip workings serving mostly local pits ran to: Dovecliffe, Rockingham South and Rockingham Hoyland on the GC Barnsley-Sheffield line, Barnsley Top Yard, Elsecar Goods, Cortonwood, Darfield Main, Wharncliffe Silkstone, Woolley and Dodworth collieries, Darton, Frickley, Hickleton, Denaby and Yorkshire Main collieries, Mexborough Power Station, Roundwood Sidings and Carr House gas works at Parkgate. Notable workings were those which ran to Brodsworth Colliery and Middleton quarry sidings via the H&B Denaby branch. On the return the 9.23am 8T75, 1.50pm

At around teatime on 13th May 1961, B1 4-6-0 No. 61066 approaches Swinton on the GC line with a short class 8 freight heading in the Mexborough direction. *John Beaumont/Robert Anderson archive*

Class EM1 No. 26004 appears to be tackling the Worsborough bank single-handed as it climbs past Lewden level crossing with a Wath to Mottram freight in June 1958, but in fact it does at least have the assistance of a banker on the rear. The embankment high above on the right carries the Midland branch to Pilley with the GC Barnsley-Sheffield line immediately behind it. *Anonymous*

8T76 and 3.15pm 8T77 Brodsworth Colliery-Wath Yard trips were allowed time at Cadeby for pinning down wagon brakes before the sharp drop down to Lowfield Junction. A class 8 pick-up came to Wath from Healey Mills via Barnsley and returned to Horbury Junction. It had a 6.8am start time from Healey Mills but was otherwise untimed.

Around 10 booked trains took the line up to Dearne Junction and the S&K every 24 hours with around 17 coming from Dearne Junction. Those to and from the Masborough direction, i.e. Toton, Carr House gas works and Roundwood Sidings reversed at Dearne Junction as outlined earlier.

An example of a local Wath trip working is 8T80 which shared the Elsecar branch with 8T81.

6.45am	Wath-Cortonwood
8.10am	Cortonwood-Wath
9.15am	Wath-Elsecar Goods
11.25am	Elsecar Goods-Wath
1.50pm	Wath-Elsecar Goods
4.10pm	Elsecar Goods-Wath
6.20pm	Wath-Cortonwood
8pm	Cortonwood-Wath

The old Rotherham, Maltby & Laughton Railway was less hectic, being open only for two shifts to pass eight trip workings from Thrybergh to Silverwood and nine from Silverwood which went to Wath, Keadby Power Station(Lincolnshire) and Manvers Main as well as Thrybergh. Only one train was booked to travel the full length of the RML - the 5.50am Worksop-Bentley Junction class 8. The only other trains booked to

use the Silverwood-Laughton section were the 6.10am and 9.5am Worksop-Silverwood and the 10.10am and 12.35pm Silverwood-Worksop. Until 1969 trip 8T65 carried sludge from Sheffield sewage works at Blackburn Meadows to a tip alongside the branch after Don Bridge East. Its working in summer 1963 was: 7.20am(7am on Saturdays) Sheffield Corporation Sewage Sidings-Don Bridge East(propelling and with assisting engine if required-35 wagons the permitted maximum,) 8.50am Don Bridge East-Thrybergh Sidings engine & brake van, 9.25am Thrybergh Sidings-Don Bridge East, 10.35am (11am SO) Don Bridge East-Ickles.

On the Dearne Valley in winter 1959/60 there were 17 booked westbound freights through area covered by this book and 14 eastbound each weekday, most serving local collieries.

All the workings mentioned so far were revolutionized in 1965 with the opening of Tinsley marshalling yard and associated route alterations so that it could be accessed by trains from any direction. No longer did the Midland and GC lines operate almost in isolation of each other with their own depots and yards(though in the 1930s the LNER and LMS tried to improve efficiency with a traffic pooling scheme.) Now virtually all traffic was sorted by the one new yard. Many smaller yards were closed, eliminating wasteful duplication and inter-yard trip working, the enormous multiplicity of trip workings almost disappearing as a result. A new centralized freight terminal at Grimesthorpe, Sheffield, replaced other local goods depots throughout Sheffield and Rotherham. Mexborough was wiped out as a freight centre, its yards and motive power depot redundant. Such yards as Bernard Road, Roundwood, Wincobank and

Mexborough West in May 1962. A Class 04/8 2-8-0 passes stored WD 2-8-0s as it makes for Wath Yard with a class 8 through freight composed mainly of empty mineral wagons. *Anonymous*

Woodhouse Mill closed while Masborough SortingSidings, Ickles and Rotherham Road were retained on a reduced scale to deal with purely local traffic - the latter as exchange sidings for Rotherham power station, New Stubbin Colliery and Parkgate steel works. Wath remained largely unaffected by the advent of Tinsley(as did Barnsley Junction) but in 1967 train working was significantly reorganized when most of the Mottram trains were replaced by block trainloads running direct to their final destinations, Mottram Yard effectively closing in 1972. Also, from about that time, traditional mineral wagons were being replaced by high-capacity merry-go-round hoppers. In the 1970s, much of the traffic consisted of MGR coal trains to Fiddlers Ferry power station, near Warrington, as well as shipping coal to Garston Dock, Merseyside, and iron and steel to Glazebrook and Warrington.

During the 1960s and 70s the demand for coal declined sharply or became increasingly concentrated on power stations as homes and industry turned to oil, gas and electricity. And the coal industry lost one of its biggest customers in the 1960s when BR eliminated steam traction. Pits began to close or were amalgamated with neighbouring pits by underground connections. The survivors were gradually equipped with rapid loading facilities for MGR operation, which BR had introduced to feed the big new power stations, where block trains of high capacity hopper wagons could load and discharge without stopping, often eliminating the need for collieries to have their own internal railways and locomotives. The great recession of 1979-81 hit heavy industry especially hard, not least the steel

industry. Age-old engineering and steel plants went out obusiness; coking plants - including the giant Manvers ovens - were shut down due to the reduced demand for coke and the freight traffic on offer to the railway declined massively.Then followed the miners' strike of 1984/85 - one of the bitterest industrial disputes the country has ever known as miners fought to save their industry. It was triggered by plans to close Cortonwood Colliery, situated along the Elsecar branch, the closure of one pit which exposed a Beeching plan for the coal industry, a government campaign to shut dozens of pits all across Britain. Many did not reopen after the strike and one by one the rest shut over the following years. Privatisation of the National Coal Board did little to save them and in 2008 Maltby was the only deep mine left working in the area covered by this book - and one of only three still winding coal in the once great Yorkshire coalfield.

The electrified Woodhead line and Worsborough branch from Wath closed in July 1981 and the remaining freight traffic was rerouted via other cross-Pennine lines. Wath Yard soldiered on for about five years after which so many pits had closed that it and the lines from it were redundant. By the end of the 1980s this once vast and bustling expanse of railway had vanished.

By 1989 not only were there considerably fewer freight trains through the whole area but their whole nature had changed. They were now mostly block trains carrying one commodity from private siding to private siding, be they pit-to-power station MGR coal or inter-works steel trains between works and purpose-built terminals. Mixed wagonload freight was catered for by the Speedlink network introduced in the 1970s. Loose-coupled unfitted trains were effectively extinct, nearly all being fully air-braked. The only vacuum-braked trains remaining were a handful of departmental trains. Traffic flows were much simplified too. There were now just two routes into Rotherham from the north - the Midland via the S&K and the GC line from Doncaster. Trains from the north or Leeds requiring to enter Tinsley yard from the east or booked to miss the yard carried straight on along the Midland either via the Old Road(now described in the working timetable as the "Barrow Hill Line") or Sheffield as required. Those required to enter Tinsley from the west took the GC line at Aldwarke Junction.

The summer 1989 working timetable showed around 30 Down(northbound) freights along the Midland line through Masborough per 24 hours - about a quarter of 1963's traffic level. In the Up direction there were around 50. It must be remembered that these included trains crossing to and from the Doncaster line at Aldwarke. They consisted mainly of block trains between steel producing plants at Scunthorpe and Lackenby and distribution terminals at Wolverhampton, Brierley Hill, Sheffield(freight terminal) and Masborough where a new steel terminal had been established, or to other steel works such as Corby, Shelton and Cardiff. Petroleum trains from Port Clarence, long-distance coal trains, cement and stone trains to/from Earles Sidings and Buxton along the Hope Valley, and departmental trains between such places as Healey Mills, Doncaster, Bescot, Toton and Bardon Hill made up most of the remainder. Speedlink services passed through en-route between Doncaster and Derby, Bescot and Stoke Gifford, Willesden and Hunslet, Tees Yard and Bescot, and Hunslet, Hull and Tinsley,

and from Rotherham to Scunthorpe. Three days a week an oil train came in the early hours from Ripple Lane, Barking, to the Yorkshire Tar Distillers plant at Kilnhurst West which, because of the much rationalized track layout, involved some convoluted manoeuvring. Arriving via the GC line from Doncaster and Aldwarke Junction, it went first to Canklow Loop for the engine to run round. From there it had to go all the way along the S&K to Moorthorpe where the engine ran round again so that the train could approach the tar distillers siding in the Up direction which was the only way it could be accessed. Once the tanks were shunted into the siding, the engine left, via a reversal at Masborough station, for Doncaster shed where it spent the rest of the morning before returning to Kilnhurst to take the empties back via Treeton, Tinsley Yard, the GC line and Doncaster.

Just 10 trains were booked in the summer 1989 working timetable to use the GC line south of Aldwarke in the Up(northbound) direction. Most were at night and half were Speedlink services, from Bescot to Scunthorpe, Newport East Usk to Doncaster, Tinsley to Hull, Eastleigh to Haverton Hill and Tinsley to Doncaster; Two were steel sector trains to Scunthorpe, one from Bescot and the other from Cardiff Tidal, the remaining three being the Kilnhurst-Ripple Lane tanks and departmental trains to Doncaster - a class 9 from Toton and a class 8 from Bardon Hill. In the Down(southbound direction) there were no booked freights on most days, the only booked daily train being 6J25, the 05.05 Scunthorpe to Aldwarke works. The one other booked train was the 06.00 Wednesdays Only Doncaster to Toton class 9 departmental. The Thrybergh-Silverwood branch had no trains in the working timetable by this

Commissioning of the new junction at Aldwarke in 1965 along with the opening of Tinsley marshalling yard changed the whole nature of freight operations not just in the Sheffield and Rotherham area but far beyond as well. Here, Brush Type 4 No. D1875 working a special southbound class 7 steel train uses Aldwarke Junction to cross from the GC to the Midland on 26th January 1967. *Adrian Booth* **As well as service pipes, the overbridge behind the modern signal box, carries a road and an internal BSC railway linking Aldwarke works(out of the picture on the right) with Roundwood wire mills visible top left.**

time but in December 1989 was despatching around 15 trains a week to the Aire Valley power stations.

The South Yorkshire Joint, carried six booked Down(Doncaster-bound) freights and five Up(Worksop bound.) These consisted of three Worksop-Scunthorpe MGRs each way, two Toton-Maltby coal workings and one return, and a Mondays, Wednesdays, Fridays Only Speedlink trip from Doncaster to the glass bulbs factory at Harworth which on both outward and return legs had to go to Maltby for the engine to run round. It should be remembered that local MGR coal trains running on any of the routes were planned on a weekly basis and not shown in the working timetable. In December 1989, Silverwood was despatching 15 trains a week to Aire Valley power stations, Goldthorpe 25 a week, Harworth 13 a week and Maltby 26 a week; traffic from Manvers Main was suspended.

In 1992 BR shut down its Speedlink network so traffic was reduced even further, what remained of Tinsley Yard was stripped to the barest minimum and even the diesel depot closed. Since then, the railways have been privatized and freight traffic through the area has changed yet again - and it is not necessarily a story of continued decline. A wide variety of freight trains still pass through the area - block steel trains, long-distance coal trains delivering mainly imported or Scottish opencast coal to the Trent Valley power stations, Enterprise services(which replaced Speedlink,) intermodal and Freightliner services, stone, cement, automotive, scrap metal and oil trains. No marshalling is done in the area now, however, and Tinsley Yard is little more than exchange sidings for a neighbouring steel works, while the only local freight sources

remaining in the this book's area are Rotherham steel terminal, Aldwarke steel works and C.F. Booth's metal reprocessors. Trains from Tyne Yard, Stockton-on-Tees, Beeston(Nottingham) and Handsworth(West Midlands) bring scrap for melting down in Aldwarke's furnaces while block steel trains run between Aldwarke and Scunthorpe, Wolverhampton, Tees Dock and the Stocksbridge works at Deepcar. Aldwarke still operates an extensive internal rail system which also links it to the neighbouring Roundwood and Thrybergh mills, and in 2009 this is the only surviving industrial railway in the Rotherham area. Rotherham steel terminal, situated on the Old Road just south of Masborough is served by block trains from Scunthorpe, Cardiff and Sheerness as well as an Enterprise trip from Doncaster.

All change

The intense concentration of heavy industry, particularly coal, coke and steel, ensured that this area's railway network survived almost intact until the 1980s, save for the loss of a few passenger services, some relatively minor closures and alterations aimed at integrating the Midland and GC systems.

These railways that mirrored each other through the Don Valley were built with no concept of overall planning as companies vied with each other for the precious traffic to come from one of Britain's fastest growing industrial regions. That was fine at the time when their only viable competition was each other but eventually road transport - trams, buses and lorries - would start taking traffic away and the railways would need to

Midland Railway Class 2P 4-4-0 No. 40409 from Hasland shed, Chesterfield, awaits departure from Rotherham Westgate on the last day of services in October 1952. The goods shed can be seen on the right. *Tom Greaves*

The awesome Gresley Class U1 Beyer-Garratt No. 69999 was the biggest and most powerful steam locomotive ever to run on Britain's railways. Allocated to Mexborough shed, it was built primarily for assisting heavy coal trains up the 1 in 40 Worsborough bank, becoming redundant upon electrification. The monster is seen here during one of its visits to Gorton Works, Manchester. *Tom Greaves*

utilise their resources far more efficiently if they were to compete.

Since 1923 the GC lines, together with those of the Hull & Barnsley, North Eastern and Great Northern railways had been part of the London & North Eastern Railway, and those of the Midland and Lancashire & Yorkshire railways part of the rival London Midland & Scottish. Through co-operation in train operating, the two big companies made some progress in better utilising the twin systems but it was nationalisation and unification under British Railways in 1948 that brought a real chance to eliminate wasteful duplication. To begin with, the whole area came under one administration from 1950 - BR's Eastern Region.

For some passenger services it was already too late. As mentioned earlier, BR axed the Dearne Valley service in October 1951. Rotherham Westgate station and its short double track branch from Holmes Junction were closed completely in October 1952, ostensibly because of the condition of the bridge carrying the Westgate station approach lines over the River Don. How the line had survived much beyond the 1845 creation of the Midland Railway has to be something of a miracle but the operating difficulties that would have ensued from trains turning back at Masborough station on the extremely busy Midland main line as well as giving the Midland a town centre terminus, must have been a factor in Westgate's surprising longevity. A short stretch of the branch from Holmes was retained to serve C.F. Booth's Millmoor scrap works and still does so in 2009. A railway presence remained at Westgate until the mid-1960s, however, the building housing the Sheffield traffic manager's Midland Lines control until it moved to the new Sheaf House office block outside Sheffield Midland station.

Passenger services over the GC Barnsley-Sheffield line which almost entirely duplicated the Midland route, were withdrawn in December 1953 and, of course, the Barnsley-Doncaster service through Wath, which somehow had never been allowed to fulfil its potential - and never would be - in June 1959. The H&B Wath branch from Wath to Moorhouse & South Elmsall closed in May 1954, the Wath station area being taken over by the NCB and incorporated into Wath Colliery sidings.

The early 1950s saw Wath at the very heart of a railway revolution - the Manchester, Sheffield & Wath electrification. Conceived in the 1920s, the project was begun in the 1930s by the LNER but delayed by the second world war. The Penistone-Wath branch was a logical inclusion because of the immense difficulty in working the almost continuous heavy coal trains up the 1 in 40 Worsborough bank. Three steam locomotives, usually O2, O4 or WD 2-8-0s, one on the front and three banking engines at the rear, would be needed to get a train up the bank - a costly and time-consuming operation, not to mention the appaling conditions for engine crews in the ill-ventilated and fuliginous 289-yard and 74-yard Wentworth Silkstone tunnels. Enginemen had to lie on the cab floor in order to breath and were restricted to no more than two consecutive shifts at a time. In an effort to overcome these problems the LNER's chief mechanical engineer, Sir Nigel Gresley, designed Britain's most powerful and biggest-ever steam locomotive. Built in 1925, the solitary class U1 178-ton 2-8-8-2 Garratt No. 2395 had a tractive effort of of 72,940lbs. It

Above: The first electric train to run on the Woodhead line. The brand new Class EM1 is hauling a Wath-Dunford test train past Thurlstone signal box, a mile and a half west of Penistone, following completion of the first stretch of the electrified Manchester, Sheffield and Wath lines in 1951. *Arthur Booth*

provided the power of two conventional banking engines and could work 20 out of 24 hours a day, but even with the Garratt assisting one banker from Wentworth Junction to Barnsley Junction, trains still took around 2.5 hours to travel the 19 miles from Wath to Dunford Bridge. And the Garratt did nothing to ease the situation in the tunnels except for being equipped with rudimentary respirators which crews had to share and ultimately rejected on grounds of hygiene.

The Wath-Dunford Bridge section was the first to carry electric trains when test running began in September 1951, with normal freight trains being electrically-hauled from February 1952. When the whole project, which included a new fully-lit double track Woodhead Tunnel in place of two single bores, was completed on 14th September 1954, it was trumpeted by BR as Britain's first all-electric main line and its most modern railway. Electric freight trains could cover the Wath-Mottram journey in half the time taken by steam, though the heaviest trains still had two electric locos on the front and two banking as much to prevent wagon couplings from snapping under the weight of the train as to assist. It was a real showpiece but within five years the 1500 volt DC system would already be obsolete as 25000 volt AC became the adopted standard.

Working the Worsborough branch was revolutionized. Electric power enabled heavier coal trains to be worked and although banking engines were still necessary, fewer engines were needed overall because unlike steam, they didn't have to return to Mexborough shed for servicing or spend down time in Wentworth Colliery siding where watering facilities, a coaling hopper and inspection pit were provided. And no longer did enginemen have to endure the noxious atmosphere in the Silkstone tunnels. The new electric locos were equipped with regenerative braking so when coming down grade they fed electricity back into the system. Gresley's Garratt was tested on the Lickey Incline and unsuccessful attempts were made to oil-fire it but also its boiler was due for renewal and, after a brief spell back at Mexborough, it was scrapped in 1956.

Various changes in other industries that affected the railways began in the early 1960s onwards, and one of the most important occurred at Aldwarke where the British Steel Corporation opened up a huge totally modern works on a new site on the east side of the GC line. It came to be linked with Roundwood wire mills on the west side of the Midland line by an internal line crossing both the Midland and GC lines on an overbridge. The 120 year-old Parkgate works closed in 1974 but in 1976 the Thrybergh bar mill opened and the old Roundwood & Dalton Colliery Railway, including its original girder bridge over the Don, was taken over by the BSC for use as an internal line from the main Aldwarke plant, BR replacing it with a new runaway trap for the Silverwood branch by building a new embankment leading to a sand drag. Aldwarke came to specialise in melting down scrap and turning it into high quality steel. In 2009 it remains the biggest, and one of the few surviving steel plants in the whole Sheffield/Rotherham area. As this book was being prepared yet another severe economic recession was starting to bite and Aldwarke's current owners, Corus, announced that, with demand for steel plummeting, 713 jobs - half the workforce - were to be lost at Aldwarke. Such a drop in production is bound to impact on the railway.

The next big changes came in the mid-1960s as they did across the whole of BR. But the Beeching closures pretty well passed the area by. Here, it was the £11 million Sheffield area rationalisation scheme which brought the most radical changes yet. It was intended to weld the twin systems into one. Central to the project, which would take until 1975 to fully implement,was the construction of the massive, totally new Tinsley marshalling yard and its accompanying diesel locomotive depot. In Sheffield, all passenger services were to be concentrated on Midland station and Victoria closed, while general freight traffic was to be concentrated on one central depot at Grimesthorpe, replacing many local depots around both Sheffield and Rotherham. Track and signalling throughout the whole area, including Mexborough, was to be streamlined and modernized. Key to these changes was the creation of a new junction alongside the new steel works at Aldwarke where the GC and Midland lines ran close to each other. The new scissors-style layout enabled trains from the north and Doncaster to enter Tinsley Yard from both the west(via the GC line) and from the east(via the Old Road and a new curve at Treeton.) It also enabled Doncaster line passenger trains to reach the Midland line, Masborough station and Sheffield Midland. Controlled by its own new signal box, which replaced the old Aldwarke Colliery and Roundwood boxes, it was brought into use in 1965 when all Doncaster-Sheffield services were switched to Sheffield Midland. Only long-distance GC line trains from York continued to use the GC to Sheffield Victoria in order to reach the GC main line until it closed as a through route on 5th September 1966. They too were then transferred to the Midland line, Rotherham Central closing on the same day.

Tinsley Yard opened in two stages - the first in July 1965 when traffic was switched from the Midland line yards, and the second on 29th October when it was switched from the GC yards. Local yards such as Roundwood, Masborough station, Wincobank and Mexborough were closed. Masborough Sorting Sidings, Ickles and Rotherham Road were retained but only for purely local needs but they would also disappear over the following three decades. Sheffield Freightliner terminal was established between Masborough and Canklow but it subsequently closed and its place taken by the Rotherham Steel terminal.

Simplification of track and signalling around Mexborough saw the Dearne Junction-Mexborough West spur closed when Aldwarke Junction opened, the Swinton curve severed and

Mexborough West, No.1 Junction and Swinton Town signal boxes closed during 1966, Mexborough Top Yard and No.4 boxes having closed in 1965 under a separate scheme. With its motive power depot having closed in 1964, Mexborough ceased to be a major railway centre, being left with only its passenger station.

Provision of a new junction connecting the Dearne Valley to the Midland main line between Darfield and Cudworth enabled most of the Dearne Valley to be closed in July 1966 along with the line to Crofton. It was reduced to just branches from the new Dearne Valley Junction to Grimethorpe and Goldthorpe collieries and the rest(except a short stretch at Cadeby Colliery and from Yorkshire Main Colliery to Black Carr Junction) was abandoned. Also in 1966, the old GC Barnsley-Sheffield line ceased to be a through route when the Rockingham Colliery-Smithywood section was closed completely. The South Yorkshire Junction Railway between Middleton quarry siding, near Cadeby, and what remained of the H&B main line at Wrangbook Junction closed in August 1967 but the section from Lowfield Junction to the quarry survived until October 1975, while the NCB continued to use the Denaby-Cadeby section as an internal line until 1981.

Between 1966 and 13th March 1969 the South Yorkshire Joint was severed from the Don Valley by closure of the Silverwood-Braithwell/Thurcroft/Hellaby section. Also on 13th March 1969, the H&B and GC Joint from Braithwell Junction to Warmsworth was officially closed after not being used for much more than wagon-storage for more than 20 years during which time it had become completely overgrown and unuseable. Then, on January 5th 1970, Sheffield Victoria station was closed and the Woodhead line Sheffield-Manchester passenger service withdrawn.

The 1970s saw relative stability but more of the Dearne Valley closed when Goldthorpe Colliery was connected to the S&K by a reinstated curve at Hickleton and the Dearne Valley-Hickleton section abandoned. Another closure, of a minor but historic railway, came at the end of 1978 when New Stubbin Colliery closed and the NCB line from Rotherham Road alongside the Greasborough Canal with it. The Sheffield area rationalisation was continuing, the most important stage of the decade coming on the weekend of 20th and 21st January 1973 when the new Sheffield power signal box was commissioned. This required Midland station to be temporarily closed and Victoria station, dilapidated with rain pouring through its canopy roofs, temporarily reopened and many services diverted there. For Doncaster and York line trains, this meant a gricer's delight with diversions via the Old Road, Treeton Junction and Tinsley Yard. Masborough station became an interchange between diverted trains and bus connections. Stage 2 began in 1981 with the aid of a £1.65 million European Regional Development Fund grant towards the £15.65 million cost, specifically to improve the movement of freight. Covering 180 track miles and taking two years, it involved extending the Sheffield PSB control area to take in Rotherham and Mexborough, replacing all the old mechanical signalling in the area.

The 1980s were a decade of momentous change that would

After 1954 the Holmes Junction-Masborough South curve only saw passenger trains if they had to be diverted because of a blockage or engineering work south of Sheffield. Here, Jubilee No. 45685 *Barfleur* approaches Masborough South from where it will continue along the "Old Road" with the 9.35am Bradford Forster Square to Bristol on 14th February 1960. The time is 11.55am, the train having taken two hours and 20 minutes from Bradford to this point, being worked from Leeds to Sheffield by 45565 *Victoria* where it reversed and handed over to 45685 before retracing its steps back to Rotherham. The curve has since been abandoned. *Robert Anderson*

leave the local rail network with the shape it has in 2009. With a destructive economic recession and the Thatcher government's ruthless attack on the coal industry, this decade saw whole sections of railway wiped off the map. Right at the start, on 20th July 1981, just 27 years after being hailed Britain's most modern railway, the electrified Woodhead line and Worsborough branch were completely closed in the face of opposition from public, opinion formers and rail unions. BR's case was over-capacity on the four trans-Pennine routes following a decade of declining traffic, especially coal, and one had to go. Because of local passenger services and freight which could not be rerouted on the other three - the Calder Valley, the Diggle route, and the Hope Valley - it was the Woodhead line that was selected for closure. It had capacity for 120 trains every 24 hours but by the late 1970s was being used by only 39, said BR, while handling the same traffic on other routes needed only 10 diesel locos whereas the Woodhead line needed 45 locos because of the changeover between diesel and electric at each end. BR also argued that both the infrastructure and locomotives were obsolete and to retain it as an electric railway would necessitate conversion to 25kv AC which was just too expensive. Opponents urged BR to take a longer-term view, saying said that a fast, direct electrified trans-Pennine main line would be needed in the future because of growing congestion on cross-Pennine roads. Being a freight only line, BR was not obliged to go through the statutory closure procedure and the

Wath-Penistone-Hadfield section closed completely

The last train on the Worsborough branch was a few empty wagons hauled by a Class 37 diesel. Two Bo-Bo electric locos then ran light from Wath to Guide Bridge for store and that was that. The overhead line equipment was removed fairly quickly but BR agreed to leave the track in situ until the mid-1980s. The Penistone power control room remained in use until December 1984 to control the Manchester-Hadfield section until it was converted to 25kv AC and control transferred to Crewe. Wath Yard survived the closure but its role was much reduced. The Elsecar branch had closed beyond Cortonwood Colliery in June 1981 and the line from Barnsley in 1983 along with Wath diesel depot. The yard was left with virtually no work during the 1984/85 miners' strike and when the strike ended, several local pits did not reopen, among them Cortonwood and Darfield Main. Most others in the area succumbed during the following 10 years. Wath Yard itself had closed by 1988 after which the 100-acre site was cleared and landscaped or used for light industry. In 1988 the 148 year-old Midland main line was closed completely between Swinton Junction and Houghton Main Colliery, Wath Road Junction having already been abolished by remodelling some years before.

By this time, only the Dearne Junction end of the spur from Wath Junction remained to serve Manvers Main but all this went upon the closure of Barnburgh Colliery and its British Coal line on 16th June 1989. With the closure of Grimethorpe

Colliery in 1993 and the big Coalite coking works and Goldthorpe Colliery in 1994, the Dearne Valley all but ceased to exist. It was hoped that privatisation of the surviving pits in the 1990s might save the coal industry but to little avail and in 2009 Maltby, on the South Yorkshire Joint, is the only active pit left in the area.

One positive event did occur in the 1980s when Rotherham Central station rose again like the proverbial phoenix. The construction of a short but significant new line - the Holmes Chord - aided by more European money - allowed passenger trains to run between Sheffield Midland and the new station. The single track line from Holmes Junction down to the GC was opened in May 1987; by May 1988 all services had transferred to Central and this time it was Masborough which closed. In the same year, South Yorkshire PTE and BR's InterCity business agreed to fund reinstatement of the Swinton curve enabling Doncaster trains to call at a new Swinton station, opened in May 1990. This gave InterCity trains a faster route to Doncaster than the GC Aldwarke-Mexborough line which then closed to passenger traffic. After that, Aldwarke junction was simplified when the Mexborough line was connected to the Midland line at Roundwood and the short Thrybergh-Aldwarke section closed altogether.

Other changes taking place around this time included the closure of Sheffield Freight Depot following a major fire and the transfer of all traffic to Rotherham steel terminal where in 1995 a train crew depot was also established with around a hundred staff transferring from Tinsley. Silverwood Colliery closed at the end of 1994 and the former Rotherham, Maltby & Laughton line from Thrybergh Junction once coal stocks had been cleared. Templeborough steel works, which once provided jobs for 10,000, shut down in 1993, eliminating the need for Ickles sidings.

In 1993 the South Yorkshire Passenger Transport Authority published its Railplan which stated that reopening the Barnsley- Mexborough line to passengers, possibly as a light rapid transit route, was to be evaluated but the idea did not gain favour, perhaps because the opening of Meadowhall Interchange means passengers no longer have to go as far as Sheffield to connect with Barnsley trains. The Railplan also suggested opening stations at Holmes, Parkgate, and on the S&K at Wath Manvers. So far, none have come to fruition.

The railway surviving in 2009 consists of the Midland main line via the Old Road and Sheffield to Masborough where the bare and disused station platforms stand memorial to past glories, and from there to the site of Wath Road Junction where it merges with the S&K to the north; the GC line through Rotherham Central to Aldwarke where it joins the Midland; the GC line from Roundwood Junction to Mexborough and Doncaster, plus the Holmes Chord, the Swinton curve, and the stub of the Westgate branch. Rotherham steel terminal is the only railway freight depot while C.F. Booth's and Aldwarke/Roundwood steel works are the only private sidings. There are no locomotive depots in the area now, even Tinsley having closed. The South Yorkshire Joint rejoices in being a key route for coal trains from Scotland and Hull to Cottam and West Burton power stations while a train a day still serves Maltby Colliery. One other survivor is the mile and three quarters from Elsecar to Cortonwood, revived as the Elsecar Steam Railway.

The new Rotherham Central is almost ready for its passengers as a Class 56 heads a loaded MGR coal train northwards along the GC line on 2nd April 1987. *Stephen Chapman*

THE MIDLAND

In the 1970s it was like passing through a gateway heralding industrial South Yorkshire - riding a Sheffield-bound express along the Midland line via Cudworth as it passed between the towering structures that made up the Manvers Main coal preparation, by-products and coking works complex.
On the south side of the line was the huge fiery monolith that was the coke ovens. Not only that, the regular coke car loco was Robert Stephenson & Hawthorns 0-6-0 fireless works No. 7847 built in 1955 which rejoiced in the workmanlike name of *Carbonisation No.1*. This photo was snatched from a passing train on 23rd June 1976 - a moment sooner and the camera would have caught red hot coke being tipped from the car and down the ramp in front of the loco.
Stephen Chapman

SHORT MEMORIES

28.12.53: Steam locos are brought in to help clear a post-Christmas backlog of westbound traffic from Wath Yard. 2-8-0s Nos. 90590, 63625 and 63669 work the 11.49am Wath-Mottram while 90340 and 63779 are on the 4.30pm. All worked via Barnsley from where another loco provided further assistance.

29.12.53: Nos. 90700, 90521 and 90538 work the 11.35am Wath-Mottram.

Sunday 7.2.54: Class EM2 Co-Co No. 27000 makes staff instruction runs between Wath and Wombwell Exchange.

8.2.54: 27000 arrives at Wath with empties from Trafford Park. The next three days see it working the 2.55pm Wath-Mottram in tandem with a Class EM1 Bo-Bo.

The Midland main line from Rotherham Masborough to Darfield was shown in the Eastern Region Sectional Appendix issued in January 1969 as worked by Absolute Block signalling with Track Circuit Block between Masborough and Kilnhurst West. Signal boxes(distances are from the previous box) were at Holmes Jn.(286yds from Harrison & Camms Sidings,) Masborough Station South Jn.(558yds,) Masborough Station North(418yds,) Parkgate Jn.(1 mile 59yds,) Rawmarsh Station(1179yds,) Aldwarke Jn.(1196yds,) Kilnhurst West South(1 mile 256yds,) Swinton Town(1 mile 317yds,) Swinton Junction(702yds,) Wath Road Jn.(1208yds,) Wath Station(1 mile 384yds,) Wath North(524yds,) and Darfield(1 mile 1454yds.) Maximum speed was 50mph on Slow lines, 60mph on Fast lines north of Swinton Jn. and 45mph on Goods lines.
Additional running lines were: Up and Down Slow Holmes-Wath Road(used by passenger trains;) Up and Down Goods Wath Road-Houghton Colliery Sidings; Down Goods Holmes to Masborough Station North. The goods lines were worked according to Permissive Block regulations while the Slow lines were Track Circuit Block between Rawmarsh and Kilnhurst West.
On the "Old Road" between Treeton and Masborough Station South Jn., signalling was Absolute Block on main lines and Permissive Block on Goods lines. Signal boxes were at Treeton Jn., Canklow Goods Jn.(1 mile 548yds.,) Sorting Sidings South Jn.(1215yds.,) Sorting Sidings North Jn.(950yds.,) Masborough South Jn.(382yds.,) and Masborough Station South Jn.(600yds.) Maximum line speed was 60mph on main lines, 45mph on goods lines and 40mph on all lines north of Sorting Sidings South.

Above: On hire to British Coal, BR 350hp Class 08 0-6-0 shunter No. 08870 shunts internal wagons at Barnburgh Colliery on 5th March 1989, just a couple of months before it closed.

Right: British Coal's Barnburgh Colliery line had a rudimentary form of signalling, as per this example guarding the approach to Manvers on 29th March 1987.

Below: Another feature of the line were these unusual buffer stops seen at Barnburgh Colliery on 13th March 1987 which could be opened up to let a train pass through. *All Adrian Booth*

Above: Wath Road Junction looking north in May 1962. From left are the GC Mexborough-Wath line passing underneath, Manvers Main Colliery, the coking plant, Wath Road Junction signal box and the North Midland line to Leeds via Cudworth, Manvers by-products works, and the S&K line to Pontefract and Ferrybridge. The posters on the right advertise Turog bread and an Easter parade at Manchester's Belle Vue zoo. *Anonymous*

Below: BR/Sulzer Type 4 No. 45007 charges past Swinton Junction signal box with an Up express on 11th July 1978. *Adrian Booth*

Roundwood Sidings. Double sided notice boards are situated at the Aldwarke Junction end of the Through and Nos. 1, 2, 3 and 4 sidings. The side of each board facing trains approaching from the Kilnhurst direction is worded "Stop and Await Instructions." The guard of a train requiring to pass one of these boards must satisfy himself that the line on which the movement is to be made is clear......before instructing the driver to proceed.

The side of each board facing trains approaching from the Aldwarke....direction is worded "Stop and Await Instructions. Telephone Kilnhurst S.B." and trainmen must obtain permission from the signalman at Kilnhurst West South box to proceed past any of these boards. A single lever ground frame is provided at the Kilnhurst end of the Through Siding to control the connection with Nos. 1, 2, 3 and 4 sidings and trains must not proceed....until trainmen have satisfied themselves that the points are in the correct position for the movements to be made. *BR Eastern Region Southern Area Sectional Appendix 1969.*

Above: With semaphore signalling still extant on the Slow lines, a Class 47 heads a Down express past Kilnhurst on 10th May 1980. The siding in the foreground leads to the Yorkshire Tar Distillers works. *Adrian Booth*

Below: Doncaster shed's B1 4-6-0 No. 61326 rattles over Aldwarke Junction on 13th August 1965 with a class 7 train of iron ore tipplers returning empty to the East Midlands, probably from Frodingham. *Adrian Booth*

Above: BR/Sulzer Type 4 "Crompton"(Class 46) No. D142 speeds the northbound Waverley, which by this time ran only in the summer, past a selection of tenders at Arnott-Young's scrap yard in the former Parkgate & Rawmarsh station goods yard(closed 1st January 1966) on 28th July 1967. The train has just passed the station which was still open, while the blast furnaces of the Parkgate Iron & Steel Company's works dominate the skyline.

Below: Awaiting its demise in Arnott-Young's yard on 20th March 1966 was BR Standard Class 2 2-6-2T No. 84019, erstwhile of Bolton shed, Lancashire. *Both Adrian Booth*

Three industrial railway systems met at Parkgate where they were in turn connected to BR. Besides the Parkgate Iron & Steel Company's system, were lines from the South Yorkshire Chemical Company's works and New Stubbin Colliery.

Parkgate Junction Sidings. The crossbar signal fixed outside the running line to the Parkgate Iron & Steel Company's sidings near the connection to that company's sidings, worked by BR guards and shunters, regulating the running of the South Yorkshire Chemical Company's, the NCB and the Parkgate Iron & Steel Company's engines, must always be kept in the clear position, except when required to be placed to Danger for the protection of BR trains proceeding on the running line to or from the Parkgate Iron & Steel Company's sidings or when performing shunting operations at those sidings.

Before any BR train occupies the running line to the Parkgate Iron & Steel Company's sidings, the BR shunter must proceed to the signal, and after ascertaining that all is clear place it to Danger. *BR Eastern Region Southern Area Sectional Appendix 1969.*

Yorkshire Tar Distillers and Messrs. John Baker & Bessemer Sidings, Kilnhurst. No engine must pass over the weighing machine in Yorkshire Tar Distillers siding....An electric lamp capable of displaying a red light has been provided on the Tar Distillers weigh office for the protection of the firm's level crossing....no movement must be made towards the firm's sidings when the red light is displayed....*BR Sectional Appendix 1969*

Above: A wondrous and dramatic industrial scene once commonplace but now lamentably rare in Britain. With the steel industry nationalized, the Parkgate Iron & Steel Co. had become the British Steel Corporation's Parkgate works. The furnaces were still in production on 25th November 1973, though not for much longer, as one of the Brush/Beyer Peacock diesels which replaced the works steam shunters moves BR wagons loaded with coke into the works. The 1960-built loco is BSC No.86, Brush332/Beyer Peacock 7939.

Below: The functional lines of the WD 2-8-0 are captured in this view of Normanton's No. 90362 as it slogs along the Slow line past Parkgate & Rawmarsh station with a Down class 7 unfitted freight on 26th January 1967. The station closed on 1st January 1968.
Both Adrian Booth

ROTHERHAM PRIVATE SIDINGS 1956

Connected to the Midland lines

John Baker & Bessemer Ltd., Brinsworth Ironworks
...also serving Harrison & Camm Ltd.
British Basic Slag Co., Ltd.
East Midlands Gas Board, Carr House Gas Works, Parkgate
Thos. Firth & John Brown Ltd.
Thos. Firth & John Brown Ltd. tipping siding, Canklow
Midland Iron Co., Masborough
...also serving Kingscliffe Super Refractories Ltd.
W. G. Moreton & Co.
Parkgate Iron & Steel Co., Parkgate works & Roundwood works
J. J. Habershon & Sons, Holmes
Owen & Dyson's works
Simon Carves Ltd.
P. Stubs, Holmes Steel Works
Wagon Repairs Ltd., Masborough
I. & I. Walker, Carr House siding
H. Whiting & Sons
Wilcock & Johns, South Yorkshire Hoop Iron Works
W. Oxley & Co. Ltd., Steel Works

Connected to the Great Central lines

Beatson, Clarke & Co.
Ben Bennett Jr. Ltd., New York Siding
Central Electricity Authority, Prince of Wales Power Station
George Cohen, Sons & Co., Coborn Works, Ickles
E. Cottam & Co. Ltd
N.C.B., Aldwarke Main Colliery
Doncaster Wagon Co. Ltd.

Northfield Siding
Rotherham Co-operative Society
Rotherham Corporation Highways Depot
Rotherham Forge & Rolling Mills
Sheffield Chemical Co. Ltd
Steel Peach & Tozer, Fullerton Sidings
Steel Peach & Tozer Marshalling Siding
United Steel Companies Ltd.
Thos.W. Ward Ltd., Templeborough Works, Ickles
Yates, Haywood & Co. Ltd

Connected to both Midland and Great Central lines

Steel, Peach & Tozer, Templeborough Works also serving...
  McCall & Co.(Sheffield) Ltd.
  Slag Reduction Co. Ltd., Templeborough
  Mottram, Sedon, Keep & Co.
  United Strip & Bar Mills Ltd.
Steel, Peach & Tozer, Phoenix Works
Steel, Peach & Tozer, Templeborough Rolling Mills
N.C.B., New Stubbin Colliery
N.C.B., Rotherham Main Coke Ovens
....also serving Simon Carves Ltd.
South Yorkshire Chemical Co.

The Parkgate Iron & Steel Co. had a connection with the GC via Naylor's Siding half a mile south of Parkgate & Aldwarke station. Also connected to the GC via Naylor's Siding were the British Basic Slag Co. Ltd. and W. Oxley & Co. Ltd.

Cricklewood-based Royal Scot No. 46142 *The York and Lancaster Regiment* **sweeps past Carr House Gas Works, Israel & Isaac Walker's private sidings and WD 2-8-0 No. 90131 near Parkgate Junction at 1.35pm on 3rd April 1961. The 'Scot' is on the 12 noon Bradford Forster-St. Pancras during what was officially the last fortnight of steam on that service.** *Robert Anderson*

Above: At 11.5am on the same day as the picture opposite, 4F 0-6-0 No. 44037 from Canklow shed heads south past Carr House Gas Works with an Up train of empties. *Robert Anderson*

Below: Steam returns to Masborough. Preserved LNER A3 Pacific No. 4472 *Flying Scotsman* heads north with the Merseyside Express railtour on 29th September 1979. *Adrian Booth*

Above: Hughes-Fowler 'Crab' 2-6-0 No. 42857 of Birmingham's Satley depot, makes a determined start from Rotherham Masborough with the 4.15pm Sheffield Midland-Leeds stopper at 4.28pm on 3rd April 1961. *Robert Anderson*

Below: About to enter Masborough station with a 1950s Up express is Leeds Holbeck's Class 5 4-6-0 No. 44857. *Tom Greaves*

Masborough Station North Junction. The points situated in the Through Siding and leading to Carr House Colliery must be kept padlocked for the Through Siding except when required to be unlocked to allow a train to work at the sidings.

When not in use the key for the padlock is kept in Parkgate Junction box and the person in charge of shunting movements at the sidings is responsible for returning the key to that box when the work has been completed and for giving an assurance to the signalman that the points are padlocked for the Through Siding.

Masborough Station-freight trains taking water. Freight trains stopping at Masborough station on the Down Slow line for water must, unless instructions are given to the contrary, when conveying more than 50 wagons, stop at the crane at Masborough Station North, and at Masborough Station South when conveying 50 wagons or less. *BR Eastern Region Southern Area Sectional Appendix 1969.*

Above: The standard Midland Railway signal box at Masborough Station North stands guard as the crew of a spotless Jubilee on the front of an early 1950s Down train await the "right away." *Tom Greaves*

Below: The London & North Western Railway was no stranger to the area, having a goods depot in Sheffield and nearly a partner in construction of the line through Rotherham Central. Nevertheless, Buxton "Super D" 0-8-0 No. 49391 adds variety to the normally Midland scene at Masborough where it pauses for water while working a 1950s northbound freight, which it has probably brought via the Hope Valley and Sheffield. *Anonymous*

Above: A true veteran, Johnson Midland Railway 2F 0-6-0 No. 58127 of Canklow shed - of a class introduced in 1875, still wearing LMS livery and its LMS number 22926 - ambles a local trip southward through Masborough station some time between 1947 and 1950.

Below: The Don and Dearne Valleys were Garratt country for apart from Gresley's Worsborough banker, the LMS 2-6-6-2 Garratts featured prominently on Midland lines heavy mineral trains. In this view, also around 1950, Toton's No. 47998 makes for the "Old Road" as it eases its train through Masborough station. The chances are that in 2009 a heavy freight passing Masborough's denuded platforms will still be hauled by a Toton locomotive - at least something hasn't changed. *Both Tom Greaves*

Above: Also around 1950, what must have then been the rare sight of a Patriot 4-6-0 at Rotherham Masborough for at that time they were all allocated to the North Western lines. Still bearing its LMS number, Crewe North's No. 5535 *Sir Herbert Walker K.C.B.*, probably purloined for the job while visiting Holbeck shed at Leeds, was subsequently rebuilt as a Class 7P with tapered boiler, new cylinders and double chimney.

Below: More usual motive power at the time - Midland Compound 4-4-0 No. 41016 of Millhouses shed, is on an Up express.
Both Tom Greaves

Above: By this time Patriots were a familiar sight at Masborough on West Country expresses. Bristol Barrow Road's No. 45519 *Lady Godiva* is filling in with the 2.31pm Sheffield Midland to Leeds stopper on 2nd April 1960. *Robert Anderson*

Below: An unidentified Hughes L&Y 0-8-0 from Rose Grove shed, Burnley, pulls up at the water column at the south end of Masborough station while working a late 1940s class 8 Through Freight. Only a handful of these engines, introduced in 1912, remained in service by this time. *Tom Greaves*

Above: Royston shed's Stanier Class 2 2-6-2T No. 40181 with freshly applied British Railways lettering pulls into Masborough with what may well be one of the Sheffield Midland-Cudworth locals. Masborough Station South signal box stands on the left.

Below: Approaching Masborough station with a St. Pancras-Bradford Forster Square express is Cricklewood Jubilee No. 45657 *Tyrwhitt*. Through the bridge on the left is Masborough goods depot which in 1956 was listed as equipped with a 10-ton crane and able to handle all classes of traffic. There were also coal drops on the Up side north of the station and public sidings on the Midland lines at Holmes Station(for coal, mineral and wagonload traffic only) and Ickles Dock which handled general goods and had a 6-ton crane. *Both Tom Greaves*

Above: A hectic scene at Masborough south end in October 1963. As 9F 2-10-0 No. 92137 gets the "right away" for the "old road," "Peak" Type 4 No. D108 passes on an Up express while a DMU enters the Down platform behind it. Beyond, a 350hp diesel shunter waits with its wagons for the gates to open that will allow it into the Midland Iron Company's works. *Geoff Warnes/Colour-Rail 1764*

Below: By the time this picture was taken on 30th June 1966, the lines on the left were the passenger lines while those on the right were mainly for freight trains travelling via the "Old Road" so it was unusual to see a freight destined for the "Old Road" on the passenger lines. On this occasion, Crosti 9F 2-10-0 No. 92029 and its class 6(continuous brake on at least 20 per cent of the wagons) block train of steel billets had been routed there to await the passage of Brush Type 2s D5848 and D5832 on a class 8 special. *Adrian Booth*

SHORT TROUSERED MEMORIES

For Adrian Booth it all began in the school holidays of 1959 when, as a callow youth, he was introduced to the delights of train spotting. His parents had just given him his first bike as a present for his ninth birthday, whereupon he was invited by an older friend to join him for a cycle ride to Rotherham Masborough Station.

"Alongside the station a connection branched off the northbound main line into the Midland & Low Moor Iron Company's premises. An ancient wooden wagon was abandoned there on a short siding and had become the meeting place for local spotters. We leaned our bikes against the wagon's wheels, before climbing up and perching aboard its top plank, which gave an excellent vantage point to watch all the trains go by. After my first session I was mystified as to why anybody would want to write locomotive numbers into a notebook, but further visits soon initiated me, I made new friends and became well and truly hooked – with my own notebook!

"Masborough Station had four platforms, with two double track main lines either side of a central island platform. Looking across from our wagon, the southbound line on the near side curved off to Sheffield, whilst on the far side it ran towards Canklow. Known as the 'avoiding line' or the 'old road', the latter was mostly used by freight trains, and we watched a procession of 4F 0-6-0s, 'Black 5' 4-6-0s, 8F 2-8-0s, WD 2-8-0s and 9F 2-10-0s working along this route. Canklow shed provided the motive power for many of these workings. Some locos were seen frequently, for example Canklow's WD numbers 90202 and 90719, and when they worked through there was frustration at not getting a 'cop' but pleasure at seeing old friends. Locally nicknamed 'Ozzies' (presumably derived from Austerities) the WDs always gave off a characteristic clank as they steamed by. The northbound line on the near side was used by passenger trains arriving from the Midlands and Sheffield, and tended to be diesel-hauled by members of the 'Peak' or Brush Type 4 classes, although other diesel classes were represented and we still had the occasional steam duties in the hands of 'Black 5s' and the glamorous Jubilee 4-6-0s. The northern 'old road' was mostly freight. A series of points allowed trains to cross over from one side to the other.

"The area immediately to the south of Masborough station was extremely interesting, with a triangle of main lines and associated sidings, which were all controlled by semaphore signals. Holmes Sidings had a resident 08 class 0-6-0 diesel shunter that was always busy. The southern apex of the triangle was Masborough South Junction, which became a favourite haunt of mine. At this point there was a fine signal box and magnificent signal gantry and, by standing there, one gained the advantage of also being able to watch all the workings on the ex-LNER line, which ran at right angles below. On one occasion I was cycling to this position when a locomotive came under the bridge and steamed towards me along the ex-LNER line. The driver leaned out of his cab and placed his arm over the second digit of his locomotive's number, laughing at the bemused expression on my trainee enthusiast's face. I was not yet accomplished in locomotive recognition and the malicious driver had prevented me from knowing whether I had just seen a WD or a 9F!

"For a short-lived period a 'Britannia' pacific was a regular visitor to Rotherham, working a northbound freight along the ex-LNER line. The precise duty cannot now be recollected, although I have a vague memory that they might have been limestone trains. Our spotting group used to vacate the wagon at the appointed time and cycle en-masse to watch a class of locomotive which was quite rare in the town.

"My favourite memory of Masborough was in slightly later days when a Crosti boiler 9F 2-10-0 came to town. I was sitting on my bike on the overbridge when a freight came down the southbound passenger line – rare in itself – and was held at signals at the south end of the station. The arrival of 92029 gave me quite a buzz, as it was the first time I had seen a Crosti in Rotherham and, as the signals were still at danger, I cycled round and took a portrait picture of the visitor. By now a good ten minutes had passed and still the locomotive did not move, so I returned to my vantage point on the bridge. Eventually the signals for the avoiding line went up and, a minute later, double-header Brush Type 2s went through on freight and I was able to take the photograph opposite. I then realised the Crosti had been held at signals because, for some reason, the Brush Type 2's had preference. I knew the points would shortly change and the 'Crosti' would cross over and follow on down the 'Old Road'. I cycled swiftly down Millmoor Lane, at the side of the Rotherham United football ground, and was soon round at South Junction gantry where I was able to get a third picture of this train!

Rotherham Central Station was nearer the town centre but I rarely frequented it. Occasional freight trains did pass through, but in my day Central was basically just served by local passenger trains running between Sheffield and Doncaster. I sometimes stopped there to note down the number of the resident 08 shunter in the sidings, but Masborough was the place to go for quality and quantity of sightings.

"Once all the local numbers had been underlined, and became commonplace, I spread my wings and was off in search of cops from further a field. I sometimes biked all the way out to Ranskill to watch Pacifics at speed on the East Coast Main line, and often travelled from Rotherham Central for glorious days at Doncaster.

"As I became a little older, train outings to places such as Derby, Nottingham, Leicester and Manchester were on my radar, whilst a favourite trip was from Rotherham Masborough on Saturday mornings when a Jubilee was rostered on the Leeds train. Upon arrival back in Rotherham I often used to call at a local shop, which was run by a cheerful old lady, and was served with a cooling drink of draught sarsaparilla. Those innocent and heady days prepared me for a lifetime as a railway enthusiast; but my apprenticeship was served around Rotherham Masborough – the young lad in National Health spectacles, woollen socks up to the knees, tank top and tie, scuffed shoes, and grey short trousers!"

Above: Looking north at Masborough Station South Junction on 30th May 1974 as Brush Type 2 No. 31148 heads a ballast train off the "Old Road" and towards the station. *Adrian Booth*

Below: Having just passed through Masborough station without stopping, Brush Type 4(Class 47) No. D1993 makes for Sheffield with the 12.15 Newcastle-Bristol in 1967. Holmes West sidings are on the left. *Adrian Booth*

The points in the Westgate siding leading to Baker Bessemer Ltd. and Slag Reduction Co. sidings must always be kept locked for Westgate siding, except when required to be unlocked for a train to work at the sidings. When not in use, the key for the padlocks must be kept in Holmes Junction box. *BR Sectional Appendix 1969.*

Right: Made redundant from its employment at Staveley ironworks by diesel shunters, Midland Railway Johnson 1F 0-6-0T No. 41708 was found stored in Holmes East sidings on 11th February 1967. Unlike the other members of the class, it was destined for a new lease of life in preservation, hence the protection of a tarpaulin over the chimney. *Adrian Booth*

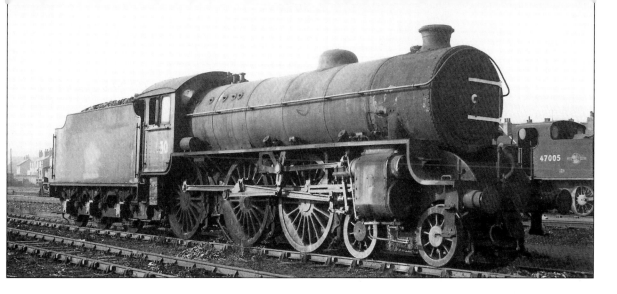

Top: The Canklow B1 4-6-0s granted an extended life as steam heating boilers at Nunnery carriage sidings, Sheffield, were a memorable feature at the end of steam. Here, departmental No. 30, alias 61050, stands in Holmes East sidings alongside 0F 0-4-0ST No. 47005, dumped after being released from its duties at Staveley ironworks. *Adrian Booth*

Right: Holmes West sidings were generally used by the engineer's department and like most engineer's yards could harbour some vintage carriages. This pair were there in June 1966. *Anonymous*

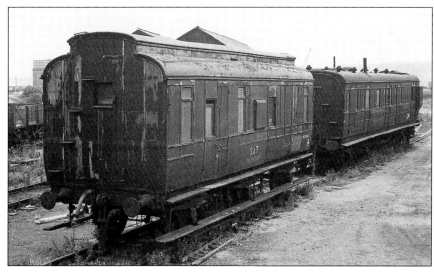

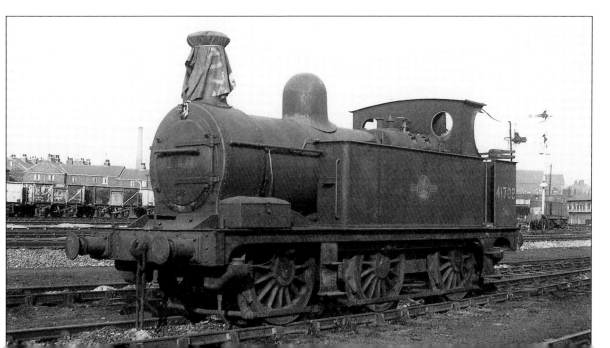

Above: Dumped at Holmes in 1964 awaiting their appointment with the scrapman were withdrawn Royal Scot 4-6-0s Nos. 46101 *Royal Scots Grey* **and 46114** *Coldstream Guardsman.* *Peter Cookson*

Below: This marvellous view of Holmes Junction shows BR/Sulzer Type 2(Class 25) No. 25043 heading a Leeds-Birmingham service on 30th May 1974. Holmes West Yard is on the left and Holmes East Sidings on the extreme right. Going round to the right is the curve to Masborough South Junction while the single track former Westgate branch trails away from it to pass under the bridge carrying the 'Old Road' to Tapton Junction via Treeton. *Adrian Booth*

Above: Passing the site of Holmes station(closed 1955) from the Sheffield direction in June 1966, a BR/Sulzer Type 4 "Peak" has charge of train 1N72, the 10.30 Sheffield Midland-Bradford Forster Square. On the right, the scrap yard occupies the site of Holmes Pottery while in the right distance was Rotherham Wagon Works. Holmes steel works is on the left and beyond the overbridge were blast furnaces and a line going left to Ickles. *Anonymous*

Below: Steam is on its way out and York's B1 4-6-0 No. 61019 has been stripped of its *Nilghai* nameplates. It is seen bringing a northbound class 8 Through Freight under the semaphore gantry at Masborough South Junction on 30th June 1966. *Adrian Booth*

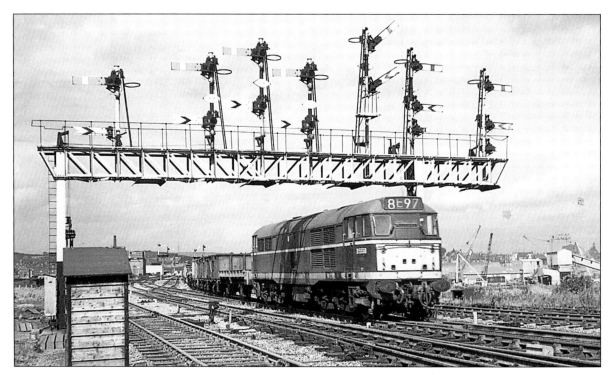

Above: One good thing about diesels was that with headcode panels we could have a stab at identifying the train. Here Brush Type 2 No. D5550 comes under the Masborough South gantry with freight 8E97 on 23rd August 1966. The summer 1965 working timetable showed 8E97 as a Saturday night Hull to Sheffield Bernard Road working via the GC line, but since then Tinsley Yard had opened so presumably it had been retimed and rerouted via Treeton. *Adrian Booth*

Below: With the headgear of Rotherham Main Colliery beyond the pylon, "Peak" No. D49 *The Manchester Regiment* and its class 7 freight are drawn up behind another train in Canklow Up loop on 8th October 1966. *Adrian Booth*

Above: Around the time of national-isation, LMS 8F 2-8-0 No. 8637 plods past Canklow with an Up mineral train. In the sidings on the right are colliery-owned wagons, the one behind the telegraph pole being lettered ANTHRACITE.

Below: At the same spot, Stanier Class 5 4-6-0 No. 5264 heads by with a class H unfitted express freight. *Both Tom Greaves*

Both the 1960 and 1969 Sectional Appendices stated that trains using the Up Goods between Masborough Sorting Sidings South Junction and Canklow Goods Junction could be shunted into the old Rotherham Main Colliery siding so that other trains could pass. The points were operated by a ground frame electrically controlled from Masborough Sorting Sidings South Junction box.

Steel Peach & Tozer's branch. The points leading from No.4 siding to Nos.5 and 6 sidings are normally set for No.4 siding, and they must be kept padlocked for that direction except when required to be unlocked for a train to pass between No.4 siding and Nos. 5 and 6 sidings. They key to the padlock must be obtained from the firm's foreman at the New Pump-house and returned immediately after use. *Eastern Region Sectional Appendix 1960 and 1969.*

Above: Also in the late 1940s, Toton Garratt No. 7989 has charge of an Up mineral train at Canklow. The Garratts were not a huge success and were withdrawn in the 1950s as soon as they could be replaced by BR's new 9F 2-10-0s. The wagon on the right appears to be lettered HOVIA.

Below: Cricklewood-based Class 4P Compound 4-4-0 No. 1054 bowls past Canklow with an Up class E(later class 5) express freight. The LMS used No.1054 to pull a portion of the Royal Scot non-stop from Euston to Edinburgh in 1928 as a publicity stunt to out-do the LNER which was about to launch its London-Edinburgh non-stop Flying Scotsman service. The extended coal rails on the tender were specially fitted for the job. *Both Tom Greaves*

On 1st October 1958, a test train of 24 Lowfit container wagons plus a standard BR brake van, all fitted with roller bearings, and with the LMS dynamometer car behind the two diesel locomotives, Metro-Vick Co-Bos Nos. D5700 and D5701, ran from London to Gushetfaulds, Glasgow, in 6 hours. The Condor container service was introduced the following year.

On 13th May 1961 a Leeds Central-St. Pancras Rugby League special took the 'old road' behind Cricklewood Royal Scot No. 46160 *Queen Victoria's Rifleman.*

On 19th July 1966, Western Region "Hymek" diesel No. D7062 passed through Masborough with a Windsor & Eton-Newcastle troop train. It returned home paired with Brush Type 4 No. D1992 on the 11.25 York-Bristol.

Above: The detritous of a railway yard is evident in this late 1940s scene. Jubilee No. 45636 *Uganda* of Nottingham shed, displaying its BR number but still with LMS on the tender, passes Canklow and a venerable Johnson 2F 0-6-0 while heading what is, according to the one lamp in front of the chimney, a stopping passenger train. In which case it is either a diverted service or one of the Sheffield-Chesterfield trains which ran via the 'Old Road' until 1954. *Tom Greaves*

Below: Begrimed Garratt No. 47984, this one from Hasland depot, heads a southbound coal train past the old Midland Railway wooden post signals at Canklow some time between 1948 and 1950. The rotary coal drum designed to bring the coal forward and make life easier for the fireman struggling with such a big locomotive, is visible in the coal tender at the back of the engine. *Tom Greaves*

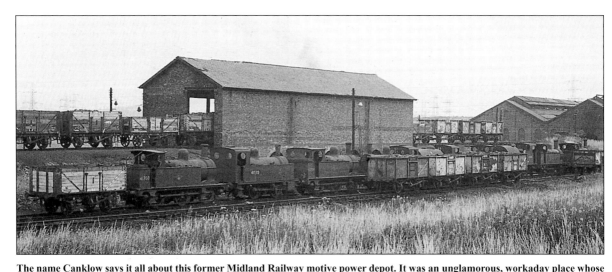

The name Canklow says it all about this former Midland Railway motive power depot. It was an unglamorous, workaday place whose prime purpose was to supply freight and shunting engines to meet the transport demands of the area's intense heavy industry. Only the odd loco was provided for passenger work though in early 1962 it received Jubilee 4-6-0s and even a rebuilt Patriot from Millhouses when that shed closed but they soon moved on to Darnall for summer traffic. Such engines came to Canklow for servicing in later years. At nationalisation Canklow was coded 19C in the BR London Midland Region's Sheffield District. Administrative changes in 1957 saw it transferred to the Eastern Region where it became 41D, still in the Sheffield District, and with the code it retained to the end.

Canklow remained fully Midland in flavour until the 1960s when an influx of locomotives from closed sheds in the Sheffield District saw it become increasingly cosmopolitan to the point of having ex-LNER types on its books.

Remaining always 100 per cent steam, Canklow lost its allocation in October 1965 when its engines were either withdrawn or dispersed to other Eastern Region depots. It continued to service visiting locomotives throughout 1966, as well as being home to B1 4-6-0s Nos. 30(61050) and 32(61315) in departmental use as carriage heating units at Nunnery Sidings in Sheffield.

Canklow became memorable as the store for the redundant Staveley ironworks tanks - Deeley Midland 0F 0-4-0Ts, Johnson Midland 1F 0-6-0Ts and Kitson LMS 0F 0-4-0STs. Ousted from their home at Barrow Hill by dieselisation they were transferred to Langwith Junction but spent their time stored at Canklow until moved to Holmes sidings for eventual scrapping(or preservation in the case of 41708) in January 1967. They are pictured above stored alongside Canklow's still functioning coal stage in June 1966. *Anonymous*

Locomotives allocated to 19C Canklow, May 1955: 1F 0-6-0T: 41805/35/75; Ivatt Class 4 2-6-0: 43037; Johnson 3F 0-6-0: 43180/1/208/25/325/463/660/4/9; Deeley 3F 0-6-0: 43814; Midland 4F 0-6-0: 43872/950/78/44002/13; LMS 4F 0-6-0: 44036/7/71/89/111/27/78/232/45/576; Midland 3F 0-6-0T: 47238; LMS 3F 0-6-0T: 47546/7; 8F 2-8-0: 48011/26/75/138/40/4/209/16/ 391/7/402/7/34/50/508/48/646; 2F 0-6-0: 58114/27/70/98/204/33/38; BR Class 2 2-6-0: 78026/7. Total: 58

Locomotives allocated to 41D Canklow, April 1965:
Ivatt Class 4 2-6-0: 43064/91/108/9/49;
B1 4-6-0: 61094/1190/1313/15/72/92/4;
WD 2-8-0: 90139/49/53/203/11/20/90/330/84/410/71/557/8/658/97.
Total: 27

Left: Barrow Hill-allocated WD 2-8-0 No. 90573 takes on coal at Canklow shed on 27th June 1965. *Adrian Booth*

Above: Inside Canklow's roundhouse during the transition from the LMS to BR. Locos in view from left are: 8F 2-8-0 No. 48140, a 3F 0-6-0 , 2F 0-6-0 No. 2997(to become BR 58170,) 4F 0-6-0 No. 4128 and 8F No. 8026. *Tom Greaves*

Below: Various aspects of Midland Railway roundhouse architecture are shown to good effect in this 1960s view of a visiting "Black Five" 4-6-0 face to face in the shed entrance with Royston 8F No. 48055. *Tom Greaves*

Above: Still with its LMS number, 3F 0-6-0 No. 3747 appears to be waiting for its driver to catch up as it simmers down the far west end of the depot yard in the late 1940s. In fact, the loco is probably waiting to go off shed as the points behind denote the outlet to the main line in the left background. Canklow had six outside roads. Apart from the main line connection, they were from the left of this picture: a through siding, the road leading through the roundhouse, the loco coaling road connected to the roundhouse road by points at this end and the shed end, the coal stage bank visible behind 3747 where loaded wagons delivered the loco coal, and two stabling sidings to the right. *Tom Greaves*

Below: Photographed from the coal stage bank on 18th July 1959, Canklow's 4F 0-6-0 No. 44111 stands on the loco coaling road as another 4F waits on the shed road. Canklow Goods Junction signal box marks the position of the "Old Road" main lines. *Neville Stead*

Adrian Booth recalls: Canklow shed was about two miles south down the 'Old Road'. It was a filthy place but Mecca for we spotters and I cycled there most Sunday mornings. The roundhouse contained a 55ft turntable, 22 pit roads and a straight through road. The last-named emerged from the back of the shed and usually had a couple of steam locos sitting there; it also provided the standard means of illicit entry to the premises. If you were lucky enough not to be apprehended by a workman, or worse still escorted to the foreman for admonishment, a typical haul was 25 to 30 locomotives, such as on 26th November 1961 which produced: 41835, 44066-089-267-429, 44828-981, 48007-060-149-151-178-389-391-467-515-539-731, 61018 *Gnu* -370, 73046-074, 90250-276-368-391-471, plus Sheffield Grimesthorpe-based 0-6-0 diesels D3086-253-698.

One day, as I approached the shed, I was excited to see in the distance a Royal Scot class standing on the headshunt. It was about to leave the depot and, scared I would miss its number, I cycled energetically up to the shed. The locomotive turned out to be 45735 *Comet*, one of the two Jubilees which had been rebuilt and – at least from a distance – looked just like a 'Scot'!

But that was nothing to the surprise that greeted me when I arrived at the shed on 7th December 1965. In front of the coaling stage were Deeley 0-4-0 side tanks 41528 and 41533, Johnson 0-6-0 side tanks 41708-734-763-804-835, and Kitson 0-4-0 saddle tanks 47001 and 47005. These exotic locomotives were colloquially known as the 'Staveley Tanks' and had been moved to Canklow for storage after their duties at Staveley Steel Works had ended. By February 1967 they had been moved to Holmes Yard, from where 41708 later went for preservation. Tragically the other eight were all scrapped.

A mid-1950s line-up of Midland 0-6-0s at the back of the shed, on a Sunday judging by the number of locos present. The front engine is 2F No. 58114 and behind it, sister loco No. 58170. Did the sand drier chimney on the left really lean or is it a distortion caused by the camera lens? *Neville Stead collection*

SHORT MEMORIES

16.9.58: Millhouses BR Class 5 4-6-0 No. 73011 and York K1 2-6-0 No. 62057 double-head a Cardiff-Newcastle express north from Sheffield.

19 & 20.9.58: W1 4-6-4 No. 60700 works the 6.40am Doncaster-Sheffield Victoria and returns light to Doncaster.

24.7.59: Trafford Park Britannia 70042 *Lord Roberts* is on the 11.36am Sheffield Midland-Leeds local and 4.11pm return.

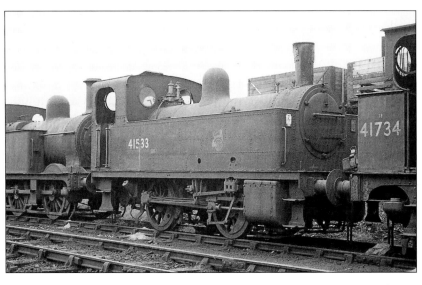

Top: An 1870s vintage Midland 2F 0-6-0 still sporting LMS number 3144(to be BR number 58233) simmers at the rear of Canklow roundhouse in the late 1940s. *Tom Greaves*

Above: Staveley tanks stored in June 1966. Deeley Midland 0F 0-4-0T No. 41533 with a pair of Johnson 1F 0-6-0Ts in the sidings beside the coal stage. *Anonymous*

Left: Another Staveley tank in June 1966, Kitson 0F 0-4-0ST No. 47005. These were not old engines, being introduced in 1932 and 47005 was one of five built from 1953 with extended tanks and coal space. *Anonymous*

Above: Around 1950 when this picture was taken, veteran Johnson Midland 3P 4-4-0 No. 40726 was Canklow's only passenger engine - and it was in store. *Tom Greaves*

Left: One of Canklow's own 1F 0-6-0Ts, No. 41875, inside the shed on18th July 1959. *Neville Stead*

Bottom: In later years, Canklow acquired several LNER B1 4-6-0s from other depots as they closed. No. 61315 was one which hung on to become carriage heating loco No.32, seen at the back of the shed in May 1966. *Tom Greaves*

SHORT MEMORIES

9.7.60: Millhouses Royal Scot No. 46131 *The Royal Warwickshire Regiment* works the 9.40am Sheffield Midland-York local, and again on 23/7.

23.7.60: Britannia 70013 *Oliver Cromwell* takes the Newcastle-Bournemouth south from York.

3.4.61: A Dudley Zoo excursion from Mexborough to the West Midlands is headed by Darnall B1 No. 61138.

The next two pages cover Rotherham's first station, terminus of the Sheffield & Rotherham Railway.

Above: A rare shot of Rotherham Westgate from the signal box shortly before closure in 1952. A Midland 4-4-0 runs round its train as an 0-6-0 shunts the goods yard. The condition of the bridge over the River Don Navigation in the foreground was put forward as the reason for the closure of Westgate which was far and away the town's most central station. *Tom Greaves*

Below: Hasland-based Midland 2P 4-4-0 No. 40337 passes Westgate's standard Midland Railway signal box as it departs the station with a local to Sheffield Midland. *Tom Greaves*

In 1922 all Rotherham Westgate-Sheffield trains but one called at all stations which were Holmes, Brightside, Wincobank & Meadow Hall, and Attercliffe Road. Journey time was 22 mins to Sheffield and between 19 and 21 mins from Sheffield. The non-stop 8am from Westgate took 12 minutes.

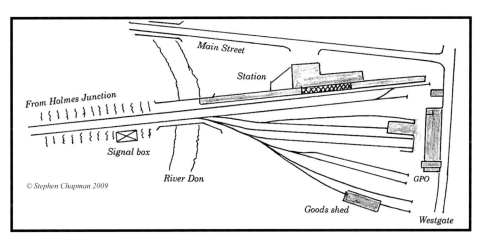

Above: The layout at Rotherham Westgate in 1903. *Not to scale*

Left: On what remains of the Westgate branch, Class 08 No. D3685 shunts at C. F. Booth's yard in 1968. *Adrian Booth*

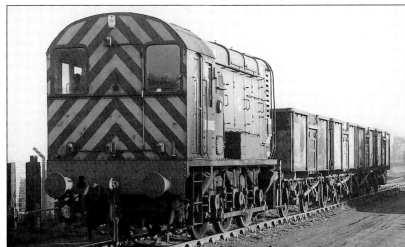

Bottom: This view of Westgate station looking towards Holmes Junction illustrates the humble nature of the buildings, sometimes referred to as "the rabbit hutch." *Tom Greaves*

THE G.C. ROTHERHAM-CONISBROUGH

Left: having just passed the site of Rotherham Central, a Class 47 heads towards Tinsley with a local trip working. A Class 08 shunter works the sidings in the background. *Adrian Booth*

A short branch to Rotherham Main Colliery left the GC line half a mile south of Central station. In 1969, long after the pit had closed, when the branch was used for other purposes, the Sectional Appendix showed it worked under One Engine in Steam regulations with a 15mph maximum line speed.

Between Rotherham Central and Rotherham Main signal boxes, were the "Long Sidings," accessed from the Down main by a ground frame electrically controlled from Rotherham Central box.

Below: Rotherham Central looking towards Sheffield in the late 1940s. An LNER J39 0-6-0 heads a southbound freight past the signal box as an N4 or N5 0-6-2T shunts the goods yard. The Westgate branch crosses over the bridge. *Tom Greaves*

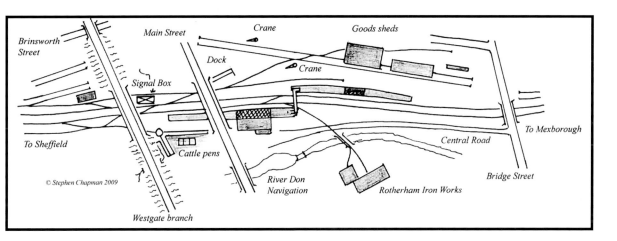

Brinsworth Street

Main Street

Crane

Goods sheds

Dock

Signal Box

Crane

To Sheffield

Cattle pens

To Mexborough

Central Road

© Stephen Chapman 2009

River Don Navigation

Rotherham Iron Works

Bridge Street

Westgate branch

Above: The layout at Rotherham Central in 1903
Not to scale

Below: Familiar B1 No. 61315, then a Darnall engine, heads a Sheffield Victoria-- Leeds via Doncaster train through Central station in early BR days. The Down side goods yard, including cattle pens, is just visible beyond the platform. *Tom Greaves*

Rotherham branch and Mexborough engines requiring to stop for water. Drivers of Up trains that stop for traffic purposes at Thrybergh Junction and which require to stop at Mexborough station for water must, on arrival at Thrybergh Junction, advise the signalman to that effect, who must inform the controller accordingly..........

Whenever possible drivers of freight trains must avoid taking water at Rotherham Central......Drivers of Down trains which are not booked to stop at Rotherham Central and requiring water at Tinsley Station Junction must give 1 long 3 short whistles on passing Rotherham Central Station box, and the signalman there must advise Tinsley East Junction accordingly.

Drivers of Down trains which stop at Rotherham Central and requiring water must obtain it unless instructed by the signalman to go to Tinsley Station Junction for it. Drivers of such trains must advise the Rotherham Central box signalman on arrival if they require to take water.

Eastern Region Sectional Appendix 1960

Rotherham Central goods depot was listed in the 1956 Handbook of Stations as having maximum cranage of 6-tons and able to handle all classes of traffic. Other public sidings were George Street Wharf (closed 1964) and New York Siding, both for coal, mineral and wagonload traffic only.

The summer 1963 working timetable showed Rotherham Central goods yard booked to be shunted by Sheffield Darnall shed's No.1 pilot from 6.30am to 9pm Mon.-Sat. It also shunted Rotherham Forge noon to 1pm. No. 3 pilot, booked to shunt Ickles sidings, was assigned to detach vehicles from passenger trains at Rotherham Central between 4.5am and 6.20am Mondays excepted. Darnall Nos. 2 and 4 pilots also shunted Ickles yard and worked to and from Ickles and Templeborough as required. No.3 pilot was shown to be immobilised from 9.20 to 10.20pm SX. By then the Darnall pilots would all be Class 08 diesels.

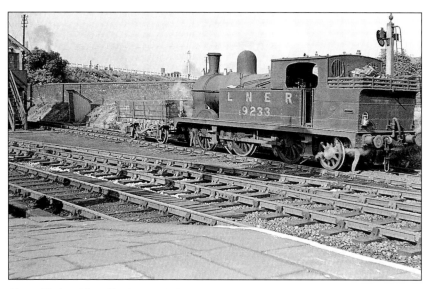

Above: Undertaking pilot duty at Rotherham Central in the early days of BR was Darnall 0-6-2T No. E9233 of Class N4, introduced by the Manchester, Sheffield & Lincolnshire Railway in 1889. Rotherham Central Station signal box is on the left and the Westgate line on the embankment behind it. *Tom Greaves*

Below: B1 No. 61174 rolls into Rotherham Central's Down platform with a stopping train to Sheffield Victoria in the late 1940s. The tones in the black and white photo suggest the loco is still in LNER apple green livery and has yet to acquire its BR shedplate which would state 36B as it was a Mexborough engine. The goods depot is on the left. *Tom Greaves*
As the nameboard shows, the station was actually called Rotherham & Masborough between 1889 and 1950, inevitably leading to much confusion with Rotherham Masborough.

Rotherham Corporation Electricity Siding. An engine stopboard is situated approximately 200 yards from the entrance to the Inwards Siding lettered "Engines must not pass this board." In no circumstances must BR engines pass this board. Inwards traffic for the works must be placed on the Inwards siding and the number of wagons to be placed beyond the stopboard at one time is limited to 22. *BR Eastern Region Southern Area Sectional Appendix, 1969.*

Right: The Prince of Wales Power Station, Rotherham, on 11th November 1973 and this little 4-wheel diesel mechanical built by Ruston & Hornsby in 1960, works No. 458952, has charge of operations at the coal tippler. The station, by then operated by the Central Electricity Generating Board, also had a Fowler 0-4-0 diesel built in 1948, works No. 4000016. The power station closed at the end of 1975. *Adrian Booth*

Above: English Electric Type 1s Nos. 20060 and 20106 pass Rotherham Road on 13th February 1981 while heading a train of 16-ton mineral wagons in the direction of Mexborough. Rotherham Road sidings, complete with Class 08 pilot, are in the background and the connections to the NCB's New Stubbin Colliery branch in the right foreground. *Adrian Booth*
There was once an engine shed at Rotherham Road and diesel locomotives were stabled there until 1980.

Below: A view of the New Stubbin Colliery line alongside the Greasbrough Canal on 20th April 1976. It was worked by NCB locomotives from the exchange sidings with BR which are visible under the bridge carrying the Midland main line along which Brush Type 4 No. 47383 is hauling an Up tank train. The line was abandoned following the colliery's closure in July 1978. *Adrian Booth*

The Great Central line from Doncaster to Tinsley East Junction was shown in the Eastern Region 1969 Sectional Appendix as worked by Absolute Block signalling with Track Circuit Block between Thrybergh Junction and Rotherham Road - the section controlled by the new box at Aldwarke Junction. Goods lines were Permissive Block.

The maximum speed on the main lines was 50mph to Mexborough and 40mph thereafter. Signal boxes in the Down direction from Conisbrough to Tinsley, with distances from the previous box, were at: Cadeby Colliery(1 mile 934yds from Warmsworth Siding,) Conisbrough(798yds,) Lowfield Jn.(1172yds,) Denaby Crossing(798yds,) Mexborough No.2(1 mile 589yds,) Mexborough No.3(598yds,) Kilnhurst Central(1 mile 494yds,)Thrybergh Jn.(1277yds,) Aldwarke Jn.(1721yds,) Rotherham Road(1 mile 765yds,) Greasborough(788yds,) Rotherham Central Station(979yds,) Rotherham Main (896yds.,) Ickles(681yds.,) Tinsley East Jn.(1353yds.)

Additional running lines were: Up Goods Conisbrough-Lowfield Jn., Down Goods Denaby Crossing-Mexborough No.2, Up Goods Denaby Crossing-Mexborough No.3, Up & Down Goods Rotherham Road-Greasborough, two Up Goods lines Rotherham Main-Ickles with no block signalling. A Down Passenger Loop at Mexborough No.2 could accommodate 30 wagons, engine & brake van and another at Mexborough No.3 65 wagons, engine and brake. There were also Up refuge sidings at Thrybergh Jn. and Greasborough, and an Up Goods Loop and Down refuge siding at Kilnhurst.

Braithwell Jn. to Thrybergh Junction was worked by Absolute Block with Staff & Ticket Block over the Down main from Braithwell to Silverwood Sidings. Thurcroft Sidings to Braithwell was classed as a goods line with Absolute Block signalling. The Thrybergh-Silverwood Sidings section was listed in Table K2 as equipped for passenger trains and was used as a Royal Train night halt. Maximum line speed was 25mph.

Signal boxes, with distance from previous box, were at: Thurcroft Sidings(2 miles 159yds from Dinnington Colliery Jn.,) Hellaby(2 miles 463yds.,) Braithwell Jn.(1704yds.,) Silverwood Sidings(2 miles 245yds.,) Silverwood Jn.(762yds.,) Don Bridge East Jn.(1 mile 838yds.,) Thrybergh Jn.(765yds.) There was a Down Goods line between Silverwood Sidings and Junction with no block signalling.

The Silverwood Colliery branch was worked by One Engine in Steam regulations with a 15mph maximum speed.

B1 No. 61315 again - this time heading train 368 past Thrybergh Junction in the direction of Mexborough. Thrybergh Sidings are on the right while the line to Silverwood, Braithwell, Thurcroft and Dinnington climbs away to the left over the second girder bridge to be built across the Don. *Tom Greaves*

Above: Brush Type 4 No. 47173 climbs up the 1 in 47 to Silverwood with empty MGR hoppers for the colliery on 9th October 1979. By this time the line went no further than Silverwood Colliery and had been singled. On the right is the tip that sludge trains from Sheffield sewage works(trip 8T65) went to. *Adrian Booth*

Silverwood Junction to Silverwood Colliery Sidings. On arrival, trains which are assisted in the rear, for Silverwood Colliery at Silverwood Junction the train staff for the Silverwood Colliery branch must be handed to the driver of the train engine. The train must be brought to a stand on the branch as soon as the assisting engine has passed beyond the miniature signal leading from the colliery branch, the assisting engine may, for this purpose, pass the Engine Stop Board. The assisting engine must not be released until the guard has properly secured the train. *BR Eastern Region Sectional Appendix 1969.*

Below: A classic early diesel shunter design. The NCB's 0-6-0 *Alex No.59*, built in Leeds by Hudswell, Clarke in 1958, works No.D1138, positions BR 16-ton mineral wagons at Silverwood Colliery in May 1977. Silverwood Colliery closed at the end of 1994. *Adrian Booth*

Left: Kilnhurst Central station and its typical Manchester, Sheffield & Lincolnshire Railway buildings, looking towards Mexborough on 3rd January 1978. Just plain Kilnhurst until 1950, it outlasted other stations along this section, closing to passengers on 5th February 1968. *Adrian Booth*
The goods yard, which closed in November 1964, was listed in the 1956 Handbook of Stations as equipped to handle all kinds of traffic but it had no permanent crane.

Right: The new erecting shop for Thomas Hill's Vanguard locomotive works under construction at Kilnhurst on 27th May 1978. Interestingly, the Kilnhurst station nameboard remains intact on the Down platform, more than 10 years after the station closed.
Adrian Booth

Left: Thomas Hill's were famous for building industrial shunting locomotives, including the conversion of Sentinel steam locos into diesels. This view inside the new erecting shop during a visit by BR staff on 7th July 1979 shows a new 4-wheel diesel hydraulic, works No. 287v, under construction, and a Sentinel diesel in for rebuilding.
Stephen Chapman

By the 1990s Thomas Hill's had been taken over by Doncaster wagon works owners RFS, now Wabtec. All work was transferred to Doncaster Works in 1993 and Kilnhurst Works closed.

SHORT MEMORIES

31.10.64: Ivatt 2-6-0s 43064/91/3 and 43149 transferred to Canklow.

16.1.65: B1s 61145/90 transferred to Canklow.

Spring 1965: The Chesterfield branch of locomen's union ASLEF claims that the remaining steam locos in the Sheffield, Doncaster and Chesterfield area are now so neglected as to be too dangerous for use on the main line.

1965: BR announces a package of 'improvements' to Masborough station ready for concentration of all passenger services there. They include replacement of the main buildings with new ticket and enquiry offices and staff accommodation with a canopied entrance, upgraded waiting rooms, and removal of buildings on platforms 1-3.

Above: Another new Thomas Hill Vanguard loco, No. 286v, being given a run in the yard on 7th July 1979. No. 286v went to work at the Elf oil refinery, Milford Haven, and 287v to Shell's Stanlow refinery. By 2009 287v was the working loco at T. J. Thompson's Tyne Dock scrapyard. *Stephen Chapman*

Below: With Mexborough loco yard in the background, K3 2-6-0 No. 61845 passes Swinton Central station with the 1.46pm Doncaster-Sheffield Victoria local on 13th May 1961. Note the locomen walking along the Up platform. Although closed to passengers on 15th September 1958 Swinton Central(just Swinton until 1950) was convenient for Mexborough shed and some trains still stopped there for the benefit of engine crews. It had no goods facilities. *John Beaumont/Robert Anderson archive*

Double-headed trains from the Rotherham branch to west of Mexborough must be assisted by an engine in the rear between Kilnhurst and Mexborough No.1. *BR Eastern Region Sectional Appendix 1969*

Above: Southern Region West Country Pacific No. 34094 *Mortehoe* leaves Mexborough station area behind and heads towards Sheffield with a Warwickshire Railway Society special returning home from Doncaster on 12th May 1963. *Anonymous*

Below: With only a couple of months before withdrawal from service, Mexborough's J11/3 0-6-0 No. 64393 - a 1940s rebuild of the original Great Central 1901 design - shunts Mexborough goods yard on 13th April 1962. The 350hp diesel is D3064, also from Mexborough shed. *Peter Cookson*

The 1956 Handbook of Stations listed Mexborough as having a 10-ton crane and being equipped for all classes of freight. Goods facilities were withdrawn on 1st August 1962. Private sidings were Bone Mill Siding, T. Burnett & Co.'s siding, the power station(then run by the Central Electricity Authority,) Dale, Brown & Co. Ltd., and Hattersley Brothers Ltd.

Situated between the River Don and the line to Sheffield, the ex-Great Central shed at Mexborough was a big depot by any standards. It consisted of a 12-road running shed, 3-road repair shop, 60ft turntable and mechanical coaling plant, having been modernised during its life. Originally coded 36B in BR's Doncaster district the 1957 management changes saw it transferred to the Sheffield District whereupon it became 41F. Predominantly a freight shed, its workload included providing engines and crews for workings from Wath Yard, including trains climbing the Worsborough bank to Penistone and Woodhead as well as shunting work. It also supplied the massive Class S1 0-8-4T Wath hump shunters and, of course, the U1 Garratt No. 69999. It had a number of mixed traffic locos on its books for fast freight and passenger work. Mexborough's allocation of 2-8-0s must have been one of the biggest in the country and in a tongue-in-cheek bid to match the glamour of neighbouring Doncaster, they were nicknamed "Mexborough Pacifics." Mexborough's allocation was run down in 1963 as main line work switched to the new Wath diesel depot and it closed completely in February 1964. The view above from Neville Stead's collection shows the depot yard on a quiet Sunday morning in the 1950s.

The summer 1963 working timetable showed Mexborough shed as having four booked pilot duties. **No.6** *(specified steam) worked at Wath Yard 1.30pm Monday to 8pm Friday. It served Elsecar Opencast and shunted the Cripple sidings 1.45pm to 2.45pm daily.* **No. 8** *was a travelling steam pilot stationed at Wath Moor Road 6am to 1.30pm Monday-Friday. Until 8.50am it worked as required Wath Yard-Wath Central goods yard where it shunted as required before clearing empties to Wath Yard at 10.30. It then placed fuel tanks into the diesel depot at 11am before working as required between Wath Yard, Wath goods yard and Manvers Main. An un-numbered pilot worked 7.30am to 10.15pm Monday-Saturday shunting private sidings and working as required. It also worked the 8.30am Mexborough-Wath Yard and 9pm return. One other un-numbered pilot shunted Rotherham Road sidings as mentioned earlier in the book.*

Below: Still sporting LNER livery in 1949, No. 1688, one of the last surviving Class B5 Robinson GC 4-6-0s of 1902 vintage, stands in the shed yard during 1949. These engines were among types deployed on Worsborough banking duty but had all been withdrawn by 1950. *Neville Stead collection*

Locomotives allocated to 36B Mexborough, August 1950: B1 4-6-0: 61165-8/74/94; O4 2-8-0: 63611/2/27/68/72/82/774/5/ 9/813/98; O2 2-8-0: 63924/7/69/70/1/2/5-85; J11 0-6-0: 64283/8/96/302/19/34/52/6/74/7/400/3/4/32/42/9; J50 0-6-0T: 68890/ 946/60/68974; N5 0-6-2T: 69264/97/314/61; S1 0-8-4T: 69900/1/4/5 WD 2-8-0: 90104/8/20/44/6/50/3/4/61/6/89/90/5/6/209/ 11/20/3/9/32/46/50/2/5/70/80/5/6/90/6/301/11/40/83/400/1/10/21/521/37/8/50/83/7/90/4/6/301/11/40/83/400/1/10/21/521/37/8/5 0/83/7/90/4/6/7/8/612/8/53/96/700/9/14. Total: 128

Locomotives allocated to 41F Mexborough, Summer 1963.
B1 4-6-0: 61138/55/67/9/1312/94; O4 2-8-0: 63645/822/43/6/50/77/82/907; WD 2-8-0s: 90149/88/90/384/400/1/10/85/91/9/ 19/21/9/44/567/72/3/9/80/2/7/7/90/612/68; 350hp 0-6-0 diesel shunters: D3060-4/329/33/697/726. Total: 47

Top: On Mexborough shed in 1948, the rare sight of a clean WD 2-8-0, or at that time ex-LNER Class 07 No. 63009 which would soon become BR 90009.
Neville Stead colln.

Right: The empty shell of Mexborough engine shed on 10th August 1969, more than five years after the depot had closed. Falling into decay in the foreground is the 3-road repair shop.
Adrian Booth

Above: Viewed from the west end of Mexborough station, Class O4/7 2-8-0 - of the variety rebuilt from 1939 with a shortened O2-type boiler including round-topped firebox but retaining the original GC smokebox - stands by the entrance to its home depot on 13th April 1962. Between summer 1961 and summer 1962 the number of O4s allocated to Mexborough had declined from 43 to just nine.

Below: Another Mexborough regular, J11/3 0-6-0 - a variant of the original GC class rebuilt from 1942 with long-travel piston valves and a higher pitched boiler - at the same spot on the same day. By summer 1962 Nos. 64442 and 64406 were the only J11s left at Mexborough and this noble mixed traffic class was on the verge of extinction. *Both Peter Cookson*

Above: One of the original Robinson GC O4 2-8-0s, Mexborough's 63611 brings a heavy unfitted freight into the station from the Doncaster direction on 13th April 1962. *Peter Cookson*

Below: First in the class of the awesome 0-8-4 Wath hump tanks, No. 69900 arrives in Mexborough station in company with an O4 2-8-0 at 5.15pm on 26th July 1952. No. 69900 was one of the original four built for the GC in 1907, becoming Class S1/1. No. 69901 was rebuilt in 1932, becoming S1/2, and two more were built for the LNER in the same year, Class S1/3. *David Holmes*
The station buildings survive in use in 2009 but apart from the two platforms and running lines all else has gone.

Above K3 2-6-0 No. 61965 of 53A Hull Dairycoates shed calls at Mexborough with what seems to be a late running Sheffield Victoria-Hull express at 5.5pm on 26th July 1952. A fish van stands in the dock on the right. *David Holmes*

Mexborough departures Weekdays 17th September 1956-16th June 1957

am
12.35	Class B workmen's train to Penistone
2.49	1.25 class A Manchester London Rd.-Cleethorpes passenger and news
2.59	1.48 class A Leeds-Sheffield Victoria passenger and parcels
4.49	4.20 class A Sheffield Victoria-Leeds
5.33 *pass*	5.0 MO Doncaster-Sheffield Victoria light engine
5.39 MX	4.52 class C Doncaster-Sheffield Victoria parcels
6.5	Class B local to Penistone
6.30 *pass*	5.45 MO Darnall-Doncaster light engine
6.49	6.20 class B Sheffield Victoria-Doncaster local
6.55	6.40 class B Doncaster-Sheffield Victoria local
7.32	7.15 class B Doncaster-Penistone local
7.58	6.10 class B Hull-Sheffield Victoria local
8.19	7.30 class B Penistone-Doncaster local
8.32	8.0 class B Sheffield Victoria-Doncaster local
8.48	8.30 class B Doncaster-Sheffield Victoria local
10.18	9.25 class B Penistone-Doncaster local
10.25	9.58(9.55SO) class A Sheffield Victoria-Hull
10.40	9.12 class A Hull-Sheffield Midland express
10.48	9.24 class A Hull-Liverpool Central express
pm	
12.13	9.30am class A Liverpool Central-Hull express
12.29 SX	10.50am class B Hull-Sheffield Victoria local

12.59 SO	10.50am class B Hull-Sheffield Victoria local
1.7 SO	12.38 class B Sheffield Victoria-Doncaster local
1.28 SO	1.13 class B Doncaster-Barnsley Court House local
2.22	2.5 class B Doncaster-Sheffield Victoria local
2.26 SO	2.5 class B Barnsley Court House-Doncaster local
3.15	2.45 class B Sheffield Victoria-Doncaster local
3.35	3.10 class A Sheffield Midland-Hull express
4.45	4.15 class B Sheffield Victoria-Hull local
5.11	4.52 class B Doncaster-Sheffield Victoria local
5.38	3.0 class B Cleethorpes-Penistone local
5.39 *arr*	4.58 class B local from Penistone
5.51	5.20 class B Sheffield Victoria-Hull
5.53	4.13 class A Hull-Liverpool Central express
6.39	6.24 class B Doncaster-Sheffield Victoria local
6.47	6.20 class B Sheffield Victoria-Doncaster local
6.56	6.7 class B Penistone-Doncaster local
7.36	4.30 class A Liverpool Central-Hull express
7.45	6.30 class A York-Swindon express
8.3	7.48 class B Doncaster-Barnsley Court House local
9.11	8.50 class B Barnsley Court House-Doncaster local
9.13	8.56 class B Doncaster-Sheffield Victoria local
9.19	8.50(8.47SO) class B Sheffield Victoria-York
9.47	9.32 class B Doncaster-Penistone local

The 1969 Sectional Appendix stated that freight trains of up to 35 wagons without a brake van may be propelled along the Up Goods line from Mexborough No.3 to Mexborough No.2 provided the movement was into a clear section. Just one wagon without a brake van was permitted to be propelled along the Up Main. Up to 15 wagons could be propelled along the Up Main from Denaby Crossing to Lowfield Junction.

On the South Yorkshire Junction Railway propelling of up to 30 wagons was allowed on the Down line from Denaby "A" to Middleton Sidings, but if the brake van was not leading only 10 wagons may be propelled and only in daylight and clear weather. The following instruction was given in the 1969 Sectional Appendix for freight trains requiring assistance up the gradient from Denaby Crossing or Denaby "A" to Sprotborough: Assisting engine to be attached to brake van by ordinary coupling which must be removed by guard with shunting pole from brake van when train has reached top of incline about 150 yards from Sprotborough Down distant signal.

Above: One of Mexborough's own B1s, No. 61166 smartly groomed for the occasion, prepares to leave Mexborough station eastbound with the Railway Correspondence & Travel Society's South Yorkshire railtour on 11th May 1952. *Peter Cookson*

Below: One of the many fascinating features of colliery railways around Yorkshire were the boat staithes where coal was tipped into barges on navigable rivers and canals for onward transport, a practice which continued until the pit closures of the 1980s. This was the boat staithe on the NCB line at Denaby Colliery on 4th May 1981. *Adrian Booth*

Above: Another Southern Pacific reaches the Sheffield-Doncaster line, this time it is Weymouth-based Merchant Navy No. 35026 *Lamport & Holt Line* that is pounding through Conisbrough station on 20th November 1966 with a Williams Deacon's Bank special to Doncaster. *Neville Stead collection.*

The original Conisbrough station had separate buildings for the South Yorkshire Railway, which owned it, and the Midland Railway which operated a passenger service. The station shown above was built by the Manchester, Sheffield & Lincolnshire Railway in 1884 but since the view above all buildings have been demolished - the Sheffield platform ones in 1986 -except for the station house, childhood home of the movie actor Donald Pleasence whose father was station master in the 1940s. The main purpose of the third platform on the right was to hold Doncaster races specials while passenger's tickets were checked before arrival at Doncaster's St. James Bridge platform. The station has only two platforms in 2009.

Left: On 12th April 1959, J39 0-6-0 No. 64747 passes Conisbrough signal box as it approaches the station with a returning Doncaster races special to Sheffield Victoria. *Neville Stead*

78

Above: The first of the trio of 0-6-0s to pass Conisbrough with returning Doncaster races specials on St. Ledger Day 12th April 1959 was J11 No. 64425 with this excursion to Penistone.

Below: With Cadeby Colliery(closed December 1986) on the left, the final one of the three was 4F No. 44414 returning to Burton-on-Trent. *Both Neville Stead*

MEXBOROUGH-WATH-PENISTONE

Mexborough West Junction looking towards Wath in May 1962. The North Midland and S&K lines pass over the bridge above the signal box while the vast Manvers Main complex dominates the scene. The curve to Dearne Junction goes off to the right. This scene in 2009 is barely recognisable. All railway has gone but for the S&K while Manvers Main has been replaced by glass and steel office buildings and warehouses. The signal box was abolished and the curve abandoned in 1966. *Anonymous*

The main lines from Mexborough No.2 to Aldam Junction were shown by the 1969 BR Eastern Region Sectional Appendix as signalled by Absolute Block with a maximum line speed of 40mph.

Signal boxes, with distances from the previous box, were at: Adwick Crossing(1 mile 455yds from Mexborough No.2,) Staithe Crossing(463yds,) Wath Junction(529yds,) Wath Central(810yds,) Elsecar Junction(1 mile 641yds,) Darfield Main(1 mile 853yds,) Mitchells Main(865yds,) Aldam Junction(420yds.)

Additional running lines were Up and Down Goods lines Mexborough No.3-Aldam Junction which were signalled by Permissive Block but with Absolute Block between Mexborough No.3 and Adwick Crossing(where only the two main lines passed beneath the Midland line intersection bridge.) Signal boxes which were not block posts were also at Moor Road Bridge(268yds from Wath Central,) "A" Sidings(875yds,) and "B" Sidings(305yds.)

Part of the branch to Rockingham South(formerly the GC line to Sheffield) - the section from Aldam Junction to Wombwell Main Junction - was signalled by Absolute Block with a maximum line speed of 30mph. Wombwell Main was 1020yds from Aldam Junction.

Wombwell Main to West Silkstone(the Worsborough branch) was classed as a Goods line signalled by Absolute Block on both lines except between Lewden Crossing and Worsborough Dale Crossing which had Absolute Block only on the Down line and between Kendall Green and Wentworth Junction which had Absolute Block only on the Up line. The maximum line speed was 40mph.

Signal boxes were at Wombwell Main Junction, Lewden Crossing(1 mile,) Worsborough Dale Crossing(747yds,) Glasshouse Crossing(538yds,) Worsborough Bridge Crossing(499yds,) Kendall Green Crossing(862yds,) Wentworth Junction(1 mile 1616yds,) West Silkstone Junction(2 miles 797yds.) An Up refuge siding at Lewden could accommodate 60 wagons, engine and brake van; a Down refuge siding at West Silkstone 26 wagons, engine and van, and a Down Goods Loop 75 wagons, engine and van.

The Wombwell Main and Wentworth colliery branches were operated by One Engine in Steam regulations with maximum line speeds of 15mph.

Above: The changing scene at Mexborough West on 5th May 1981. Brush Type 4 No. 47221 comes under the North Midland/S&K lines with an eastbound MGR coal train. The signal box is long gone and the formation of the curve to Dearne Junction has been filled in. Adwick Crossing can just be made out at the foot of the Manvers Colliery headgear. *Adrian Booth*

Below: A "Peak" Type 4 hurries north along the North Midland line past Wath Road Junction in May 1962. Below is Mexborough West Junction looking east. Following abolition of the junction and signal box in 1966, control of the transition from four to two running lines came under Mexborough No.3. *Anonymous*

Left: The NCB cabin, ground frame and "Await Instructions" board at Manvers Main on 30th May 1981. *Adrian Booth*

Below: Austerity 0-6-0ST No. 49 *Ted*, built by Hunslet in 1950, works No. 3701, draws BR 16-ton mineral wagons over the weighbridge at Manvers Main on 5th May 1970. *Adrian Booth*

Manvers Main Washery BR Empties Branch. The branch line between the National Coal Board Empties sidings at Manvers Washery and the Eastern Region main lines at Wath Central Junction is known as the Eastern Region Empties Branch....Access to this line is gained via connections with the Up and Down Goods lines approximately 290 yards west of Wath Central Junction signal box and trains are admitted to the branch under the authority of the signalman at that point.

Empty trains proceeding over the branch must come to a stand in the run-round road; and the brake van brought next to the engine, the train must then be drawn forward into the spur giving access to the Empties Sidings curve.......The guard in charge of movements on the Empty Sidings curve must, before authorising the movements to pass the stop boards situated on either side of the level crossing, obtain the permission of the NCB crossing keeper and observe that the barriers have been closed to road traffic.......When the Empties Sidings shunter has set the points for the sidings concerned and is in a position to accept the train, he will advise the guard by telephone that the propelling movement may commence along the Empties Sidings curve into the Empties Sidings, after which the guard will give a hand signal to the driver to indicate that the train may pass the "Wait Instructions" board located at the points connecting the spur with the Empties Sidings curve.

After disposing of the train in the Empties Sidings, the engine and brake van must proceed over the ER and London Midland Region running line to the LMR Loaded Sidings Ground Frame signals and when the latter are lowered, from thence to the Washery sidings....the movement must continue along the ER running road as far as the ER Loaded Sidings stop board which must only be passed under the authority of the Loaded Sidings Shunter. Eastern region loaded trains must only leave the sidings via the existing Manvers Washery ground frame. *Eastern Region Sectional Appendix 1969. It is presumed that London Midland Region refers to the North Midland line.*

SHORT MEMORIES

8.4.67: A Grimsby-Aintree Grand National special hauled by Type 3 No. D6818 runs via Mexborough and the now freight only line through Rotherham Central to Sheffield Victoria where D6818 hands over to an EM1 electric.

9.4.67: Departmental B1s Nos. 30 and 32, formerly at Canklow shed, are noted on Royston depot.

1.11.68: The 11.05 Hull-Sheffield DMU arrives at Mexborough propelled by Class 47 No. 1520 after failing soon after Doncaster. No. 1520 then runs round the unit and hauls it to Sheffield, arriving 45 minutes late.

23.12.68: Flooding badly damages an embankment on the Worsborough branch. Trains are diverted via Barnsley, usually with two diesels plus the electric on the front and another diesel banking at the rear up the 1 in 41 climb from Barnsley to Summer Lane.

Above: One of the Rumanian-built Class 56s, No. 56023, overtakes 350hp shunters Nos. 08866 and 08050 as it passes Wath Central Junction with MGR hoppers bound for Wath Yard on 14th March 1978. *Adrian Booth*

Below: Wath Central station looking east, still intact and complete with enamel nameboard on the side of the building on 27th May 1978, 19 years after closure. Originally Wath, the station was called Wath-on-Dearne from 1907 until 1950. *Adrian Booth*
Wath Central goods yard was listed in the 1956 Handbook of Stations as equipped with a 5-ton crane and able to handle all classes of freight. After closing on 1st March 1965, it became W. George's scrapyard where a number of BR steam locos were broken up.

Engines which are used to propel wagons over the Down Goods line from Wath Station box towards Elsecar Junction may.....return to Wath Station box in the facing direction. A Train Staff is provided lettered "Facing road working on Down Goods line Elsecar Junction to Wath Station" and this Train Staff will be handed to the driver by the signalman at Wath Station box before the engine leaves for...Elsecar Junction.
An engine must not return in the facing direction unless the driver is in possession of this Train Staff.......*Eastern Region Sectional Appendix 1969*

Above: Staple power for the Penistone-Doncaster trains but not after this day. Class C14 4-4-2T No. 67445 calls at Wath Central with such a train on 27th June 1959, the last day of local passenger services. *Neville Stead*

The 1956 Handbook of Stations listed the following private sidings at Wath: NCB Manvers Main Colliery, coke ovens and washery; NCB Wath Main Colliery and coke ovens, connected to the GC between Wath Central and Elsecar Jn.; Thos. W. Ward Ltd., connected to the GC at Wath Central; and Waterstone Glassware Co., connected to the Thos.Ward siding.

Below: A private siding appearing since the 1956 Handbook of Stations listing was William Pepper & Sons who operated the Wath and Elsecar screens on behalf of the NCB's Opencast Executive. Pepper's engine there on 31st March 1968, sporting the company's orange and black livery, was ex-BR 3F 0-6-0T No. 47445. Better known for its work at the British Oak staithes at Crigglestone, near Wakefield, it moved to Wath in June 1967 but was back at Crigglestone by 1969. *Adrian Booth*

Above: Class 08 350hp 0-6-0 shunters 08047 and 08051 enter Wath Yard with a coke train, almost certainly from Manvers Main on 7th March 1978. The NCB internal wagons across the other side of the field are in the yard of what used to be the Hull & Barnsley Railway's terminus, the station buildings visible behind the wagons to the right. *Adrian Booth*

Below: Another coke train in Wath Yard, this one in the late 1950s attached to Class EM1 Bo-Bo No. 26030. *Tom Greaves*

Above: The scene at Wath electric shed looking west on 27th November 1976. The Class 76 EM1 Bo-Bo electrics stabled there are Nos. 76036/52/49/26/08/31/28/24/12 and 76003. An English Electric Type 3(Class 37) diesel stands outside the shed while a Class 08 shunter lurks inside. *Adrian Booth*

The motive power needs of Wath Yard and the lines radiating from it were traditionally met by Mexborough steam shed but when the Manchester, Sheffield and Wath lines were electrified in the early 1950s, a new two-road electric loco maintenance and inspection shed was built on the north side of the main running lines at the Wath station end of the yard. When boundary changes in 1957 transferred electric loco maintenance to the London Midland Region the depot was eventually used for diesel inspection and fuelling though electrics continued to be stabled there. The view above is the well known one of Wath depot but around 1963 a new three-road diesel maintenance shed was built amid the yards on the south side of the main lines and Wath(then 41C) received an allocation of main line diesels to replace the Mexborough-based steam locos. It was an allocation which grew over the ensuing years to more than 70. But the glory was short-lived. By 1970 Wath had lost its main line allocation and was left with only its shunters.

Its diesel allocation was mainly for trip working to and from collieries around the area but its locos could also travel further afield. One notable Wath diagram until the 1970s was the 01.12 and 01.17 Manchester Piccadilly to Cleethorpes newspaper trains, one carrying passengers until 1970, after which it(the 01.17) only carried passengers east of Doncaster. Light engines left Wath depot at 00.30 and 01.05 for Penistone where they took over the respective trains. On Mondays a third light engine left Wath at 01.48 for Barnsley Exchange where it was used to detach vans from the 01.12. The depot only just survived the MSW closure in July 1981, itself closing in 1983.

Wath depot had five pilot duties in summer 1963. Nos. 1 and 2 worked 6am to 10pm Monday to Saturday at "A" hump, Nos. 4 and 5 worked the same hours at "B" hump. One unnumbered duty worked at Barnsley 2.25am to 9.10pm Monday-Saturday and 2.15am to 3am Sunday. It began by detaching a van off the 01.17 Manchester-Cleethorpes news and then shunted all goods depots as required. It also worked a 3.10pm SO Barnsley-Wath trip and 5.40pm return.

Locomotives allocated to 41C Wath.
Summer 1963.
Brush Type 2: D5527/8/38/9/42/83/4/5/5804-28. Total 33.

November 1966.
350hp 0-6-0: D3060/1/2/3/4/329/33/726/4031/2/3. Brush Type 2: D5679/5811-34/6/7/8/9/42/56. English Electric Type 3: D6746/7/6959-68. Sulzer Type 2: D7624-44.   Total 75.

November 1977(depot code now WH)
350hp 0-6-0: 08047/8/9/50/1/870. Total: 6

Above: When Wath's main line diesel allocation was at its peak. Class 08 shunters D4034(left) and D3060 keep company at the former electric shed with newly delivered Class 25s Nos. D7631 and D7637 on 25th June 1966. *Adrian Booth*

Wath diesel depot: Drivers must obtain the permission, by telephone, of the pointsman at "A" or "B" cabin, as the case may be, prior to leaving the depot towards the cabin concerned. *BR Eastern Region Sectional Appendix, 1969*

Below: Views of the three-road diesel maintenance shed are rare. This one shows Brush Type 4(Class 47) No. D1552 and brake tender in the shed as English Electric Type 3s(Class 37) Nos. D6807 and D6818 stand alongside on 12th September 1964. Wath itself had an allocation of Brush Type 4s for a short time in late 1965/early 1966. *Gerry Firth*

Above: The Great Central had four mighty 0-8-4 tank locomotives specially built for hump shunting at Wath Yard. Its successor, the LNER, classed them S1, rebuilt one(Class S1/2) had another two built in 1932(Class S1/3.) This early 1950s view shows seriously workstained S1/3 No. 69905, one of the LNER pair, simmering at the steam loco servicing point during a break in its arduous duties.

Below: S1/1 No. 69903 on Wath hump duty. The S1s worked at Wath until replaced by some of the country's first Class 08 diesel shunters, Nos. 13060-64(later D3060-64)which were allocated to Mexborough until being transferred to Wath diesel depot when Mexborough closed. The same diesels shunted and performed trip work at Wath until the run-down of the early 1980s. The signal box is beyond identification but the location suggests Wath Sidings 'B.' *Both Tom Greaves*

Below: Heading a line of stabled electrics at Wath in the early 1960s is the prototype Class EM1 No. 26000 *Tommy*. Built at Doncaster in 1941 as No. 6701, becoming No. 6000 under the LNER's 1946 renumbering, it was sent for trials on the Netherlands Railways in 1947. It returned to Britain in 1952 and was officially named *Tommy*, a name affectionately bestowed on it by the Dutch as a mark of their gratitude to British forces who liberated them from the Nazis.

Slightly different in design to the rest of the class, which were built at Gorton between 1950 and 1953, *Tommy* was withdrawn in the late 1960s and, despite its historical value, was scrapped. No. 76020(formerly 26020) was preserved and is now in the National Railway Museum at York. *Tom Greaves*

Bottom: Tinsley-based English Electric Type 3 No. 37126 leaves Wath Yard with a westbound train of empty 16-ton mineral wagons on 6th March 1978. *Adrian Booth*

Above: At the western end of Wath Yard was Elsecar Junction where the branch to Corton-wood and Elsecar diverged southwards from the Mexborough-Barnsley line. One of Wath's long-serving 350hp diesel shunters, No. 08050(former D3063,) pauses on the level crossing during a shunting movement on 7th March 1978. *Adrian Booth*

Below: The yard at Cortonwood Colliery on 17th August 1985 with the NCB's ex-BR Drewry Class 04 0-6-0 diesel shunter No. D2328 by the weighbridge house. Withdrawn from Gateshead shed in 1968, D2328 went to Dinnington Colliery in 1969 and worked at other pits before reaching Cortonwood. The colliery closed in 1985 and a year later the site had been cleared. *Adrian Booth*

SHORT MEMORIES

22.1.69: Deltic No. 9018 *Ballymoss* passes through Mexborough with a night-time Leeds-Doncaster-Sheffield parcels.

21.6.69: Preserved A3 Pacific No. 4472 *Flying Scotsman* takes a Doncaster-Cleethorpes railtour via Huddersfield, Penistone, Barnsley, Mexborough and Rotherham Central.

Summer 1969: The minister of Transport approves the withdrawal of passenger services between Penistone and Hadfield, Penistone Barnsley Jn. and Barnsley Station Jn., and Barnsley Quarry Jn. and Mexborough No.2.

29.2.72: Class 47 No. 1520 comes to the rescue again when it pushes the 07.40 Sheffield-Leeds into Rotherham Masborough after "Peak" No. 184 fails.

Above: Having arrived at Wath with the Locomotive Club of Great Britain's Great Central Rail Tour of 3rd September 1966, Wakefield B1 4-6-0s Nos. 61173 and 61131 wait to hand over to Class EM1 No. E26021 for the run up the Worsborough bank to Penistone, Woodhead and Manchester. *Jack Wild/Stephen Chapman archive*

Below: The rare sight of a passenger train at Elsecar Goods, terminus of the Wath-Elsecar branch. J11 0-6-0 No. 64374 on RCTS railtour duty awaits its passengers for the return journey on 7th June 1953. The chimney marks the Earl Fitzwilliam's iron works. *B.G. Tweed/Peter Cookson collection*

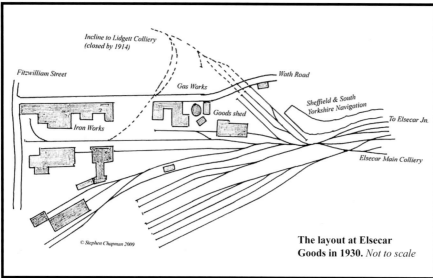

Incline to Lidgett Colliery (closed by 1914)

Fitzwilliam Street

Gas Works

Iron Works

Goods shed

Wath Road

Sheffield & South Yorkshire Navigation

To Elsecar Jn.

Elsecar Main Colliery

© Stephen Chapman 2009

The layout at Elsecar Goods in 1930. *Not to scale*

Above: Elsecar branch terminus on 19th February 1978, looking from the colliery towards the goods station and ironworks. *Adrian Booth.*

The 1956 Stations Handbook listed Elsecar as "Elsecar East," stating that it had a 5-ton crane and was equipped to handle general goods plus "parcels and miscellaneous traffic." By then there was no connection to the ironworks, the only private sidings being the colliery and the NCB's Central Workshops.

Elsecar East, as it had been known since 1951, closed in December 1963 but the branch continued to serve Elsecar Main Colliery until it closed along with Cortonwood in the 1980s.

Elsecar Goods was how the 1969 Eastern Region Sectional Appendix described the Elsecar branch terminus. It was signalled by Absolute Block from Elsecar Junction to Cortonwood. The one intermediate signal box was at Cortonwood(1534yds from Elsecar Junction.) It was another 1 mile 1430yds from Cortonwood to the end of the branch. Maximum line speed was 15mph.

The Sectional Appendix stated: "The Elsecar branch....is open from 06.00 until traffic is cleared. The branch main line between Cortonwood and the stop board adjacent to overbridge No.40 is worked in accordance with "One Engine in Steam" regulations.....The section of the branch between the stop board at Bridge No.40 and the stop board adjacent to the spring points from branch to colliery sidings is under the supervision of the BR shunter in charge of Elsecar Yard. NCB engines must not be allowed to foul or run upon this section of the line except under personal supervision of the BR shunter. The section beyond the stop board adjacent to the spring points to Elsecar goods yard may be used by NCB engines except when restricted by the BR shunter....The BR shunter must not permit any movement of BR engines or vehicles past the stop board adjacent to the spring points into Elsecar goods yard nor must any movement be made to or from the NCB Loaded siding, empties branch or loop until he has come to a proper understanding with the NCB shunter." The Appendix also stated that level crossing gates at Hemingfield and Tingle Bridge must be opened by the fireman and closed by the guard, and similarly at Mapplebeck before 06.00 and after 20.00.

Above: Elsecar Main Colliery on 11th March 1981 with NCB 0-6-0 diesel hydraulic *Wilf No. 72* built by Hunslet Engine Co. in 1965(works No. 6287) shunting the yard. In the 1970s it shared the work at Elsecar with Hunslet No. 6230 built in 1964 and named *Walter No.69*. The use of NCB locomotives at Elsecar ceased in September 1981 and *Wilf No. 72* was transferred to Cortonwood.

Below: NCB Rolls Royce 0-4-0 diesel hydraulic No. 10203, built 1965, at the head of a rake of MGR hoppers being loaded at Darfield Main Colliery on 5th June 1979. Rail traffic did not resume here when the miners' strike ended in 1985, coal thereafter being wound at Grimethorpe. *Both Adrian Booth*

Darfield Main. Guards in charge of trains to be propelled into Darfield Main Colliery sidings must ascertain that the train can be accommodated in the sidings and advise the signalman at Darfield Main signal box accordingly.
Drivers of trains to be propelled from the Up Goods line into Darfield Main Colliery sidings must not commence the propelling movement until the Klaxon horn, situated in the vicinity of the Up Sidings Ground Frame and operated by Darfield Main signal box, sounds.
BR Eastern Region Southern Area Sectional Appendix 1969.

Above: An early 20th century view of Wombwell station and its buildings of standard MS&L design. Renamed Wombwell Central in 1950, it closed to passengers when local services were withdrawn on 29th June 1959. The goods yard, closed from 6th January 1964, was listed in the 1956 Stations Handbook as able to handle just general goods and livestock. It had no permanent crane. *Stephen Chapman archive*

Guards of Up trains requiring to shunt at or place wagons in Wombwell Central goods yard must not commence such movements until No.1 lever in the ground frame is operated. Guards of trains arriving on the Up Goods line to work in Wombwell Central goods yard must not use the crossover Up Goods to Down Goods, unless permission has been obtained from the signalman at Wombwell Central...Guards of Down trains requiring to shunt at Wombwell Central goods yard must obtain the permission of the signalman...before Nos.1 and 3 levers in the ground frame and the crossover points are operated.

Movements to or from Wombwell Central goods yard must only take place when Wombwell Central signal box is open(8am-3.30pm Mon-Fri and to 11.30am Sat - *sic.)*
Eastern Region Sectional Appendix 1960.

Below: On the Worsborough branch. A Class EM1 banking engine descends to Wombwell Main past Lewden level crossing in the 1950s. *Anonymous*

LEWDEN CROSSING

Drivers of the front engine of Down trains .... over the Worsborough branch and which are assisted by an engine in the rear, must shut off steam after passing Wombwell Main Jn. and apply the hand brake slightly, leaving propulsion of the train to the rear engine, so that the driver of that engine shall have no difficulty in keeping it close up to the brake van.....

Through trains from Rotherham branch to Barnsley Jn. and west thereof which are conveying the same number of wagons as a double load from Wath to the west must be worked by one engine only in front from the Rotherham branch to Elsecar Jn. and be assisted in the rear from Kilnhurst to Mexborough No.1.

Double-headed trains Wath to Dunford and west thereof must be worked without additional assistance from Aldam Jn. to Wombwell Main Jn.. provided there is a clear road from Mitchell Main Down Home signal to Lewden Crossing. *BR Sectional Appendix 1969*

Below: This view from the cab of an electric loco descending the bank past Lewden Crossing c1954 shows EM2 Co-Co No. 27001 coming the other way while on a driver training run. Seven EM2s were built for express passenger work between Manchester and Sheffield but were run on the line to Wath prior to completion of the Woodhead line electrification. *Tom Greaves*

Above: EM1 No. 76003 comes down the bank past Kendall Green Crossing with a mixed freight on 7th September 1978.
Stephen Chapman

Wentworth Colliery single line........Moveable derailers are provided at the signal box end of Nos. 1 and 2 East Loaded sidings and guards must ensure these have been removed from the rails before a train movement is made in or out of the sidings and replaced when the movement has been completed. *Supplement issued 1970 to BR Eastern Region 1969 Sectional Appendix.*

Below: A pair of EM1s, Nos. 76032 and 76034 emerge from one of the Silkstone tunnels on the slog up the Worsborough incline with an MGR coal train bound for Fiddlers Ferry power station, Warrington, on 26th February 1981. *Adrian Booth*

Above: Ex-North Eastern Railway Class EF1 electric locos from the Newport-Shildon line, de-electrified in 1935, were earmarked for banking duties on the Worsborough branch and No. 11 seen here was rebuilt at Doncaster Works in 1941 for this purpose and, becoming BR No. 26510, was classed EB1(Electric Banker 1.) In the event the EM1s were chosen and the modified loco - seen here at Doncaster - was sent south to Ilford car sheds in Essex where, as departmental No. 100, it was depot shunter until withdrawn in 1960.

Below: The rest of the NER electrics were officially withdrawn in 1950 and broken up at Wenty's scrap yard at Catcliffe, near Rother-ham, where Nos. 26507 and 26509 are pictured. The differences between these original locos and the modified version above include the replacement of two pantographs with one. *Both Tom Greaves*

Above: Class 76s Nos. 76023 and 76029 cross Oxspring Viaduct, between West Silkstone Junction and Barnsley Junction with a freight to Wath on 6th July 1976. *Adrian Booth*

Below: Barnsley Junction, Penistone, with the sidings on the right, as seen from the cab of a Rotherwood(Sheffield)-Garston Dock coal train on 19th August 1980. The oncoming pair of Class 76s are running light, Penistone station is in the right distance and the David Brown foundry on the left. *Stephen Chapman*

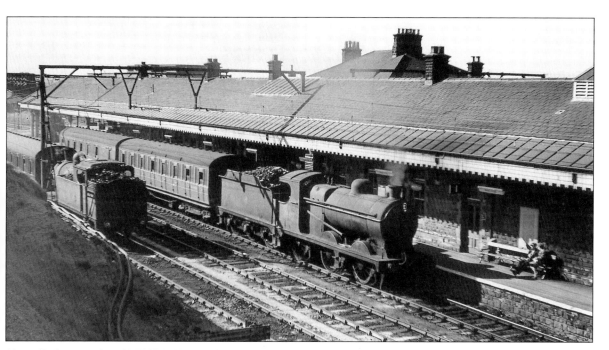

Above: Penistone station with J11/3 0-6-0 No. 64417 awaiting departure on the 5.30pm Saturdays Only to Barnsley Court House on 23rd May 1959. A C14 4-4-2T stands in the siding with its train. *David Holmes*

Below: Thurlstone, west of Penistone, and a WD 2-8-0 forges its way through the January 1947 snow towards Woodhead with a west-bound coal train. *Arthur Booth*

Right: Pre-electrification Great Central power on the Woodhead line. LNER B5 4-6-0 No. 5475 has steam to spare as it works hard past Shore Hall, Thurlstone, with an express in 1946. *Arthur Booth*

Below: At Crow Edge, about five miles west of Penistone, was the Hepworth Iron company's works(actually making clayware pipes) which was connected to the Woodhead line at Hazlehead by its own branch negotiating a tunnel on the way. In this early 1950s view, one of the company's 0-6-0 tanks leaves the works and heads for the main line.

The better-known loco here was the very attractive 0-6-0T *Hepworth* built by the Yorkshire Engine Co. at Meadow Hall in 1905, works No. 799.

Tom Greaves

THE DEARNE VALLEY RAILWAY

Above: After the replacement of L&Y 2-4-2 tanks with Ivatt Class 2 2-6-2Ts, an auto-train awaits departure at Grimethorpe Halt on 18th August 1951.

Below: Ivatt Class 2 2-6-2T No. 41250 of Wakefield shed, calls for water at Grimethorpe Colliery sidings while on passenger duty on 18th August 1951. *Both N.E. Stead collection*

Left: A near-derelict coach body was the best accommodation that the Dearne Valley could provide for its passengers at Harlington Halt, seen here just before closure. It was much the same at other stations along the line. *Neville Stead collection*
Goods facilities survived at Harlington until March 1956 and at Goldthorpe & Thurnscoe until January 1954.

The BR North Eastern Region working timetable from 2nd November 1959 to 12th June 1960 showed the Grimethorpe-Yorkshire Main Colliery sidings, Edlington, section of the Dearne Valley as carrying 14 booked freights in the Down direction on Mondays to Fridays. All were class J unfitted mineral trains mostly out and back workings from Crofton Hall sidings, Wakefield, and all but one of the Down trains ran to Crofton Hall.

They originated from Hickleton, Frickley(S&K,) Goldthorpe, Houghton, Yorkshire Main, Markham Main, Rossington, and Firbeck collieries. Two trains started from Black Carr sidings, Doncaster, and one from Kirkby sidings, Notts., which had presumably travelled via the South Yorkshire Joint. The 12.30pm from Goldthorpe went to Brierley Jn. on the H&B.

In the Up direction there were 12 trains plus engine & brake van movements - the 8.7am Wakefield shed-Barnburgh, the 12 noon ThO Brierley Jn.-Denaby Sidings, and the 1.45pm Brierley Jn.-Goldthorpe. Trains were almost entirely class H empties running to the collieries and yards where the Down trains originated from.There were no booked freights on Saturday afternoons and none on Sundays.

Below: A coal train near Harlington Halt, Barnburgh, on 18th August 1951 with Fowler 7F 0-8-0 No. 49620 in charge. *Neville Stead collection*

Goldthorpe & Thurnscoe departures summer 1939

am		
8.52	8.10	Wakefield-Edlington
9.40	9.18	Edlington-Wakefield
11.7	10.25	Wakefield-Edlington
11.55	11.33	Edlington-Wakefield
pm		
1.47	1.5	Wakefield-Edlington
2.34	2.13	Edlington-Wakefield

4.32 *arr*	3.50 from Wakefield
4.40	4.40 to Wakefield
6.27	5.45 Wakefield-Edlington
7.17	6.50 Edlington-Wakefield
8.57 SO	8.15 from Wakefield
9.5 SO	9.5 to Wakefield
10.18 SO	10.6 from Wakefield
10.57 SO	10.57 to Wakefield

Left: A very smart looking Denaby Sidings signal box on 22nd August 1952.
There was a passenger halt here which closed on 1st January 1949 but no public goods facilities.
Neville Stead collection

Signal boxes and other points on the DV in 1959 with mileage from Bessacar Jn., Doncaster, were: Yorkshire Main Sidings(3 miles 43yds,) Edlington (4 miles 20yds,) Denaby Sidings(7 miles 29yds,) Barnburgh(9 miles 30yds,) Goldthorpe Colliery (9 miles 75yds,) Hickleton Colliery(10 miles 52yds,) Thurnscoe Jn.(11 miles 35yds,) Houghton Sidings(14 miles 3yds,) Grimethorpe Sidings(14 miles 47yds,) Shafton Jn.(17 miles 2 yds,) Crofton Hall(21 miles 47yds.)

Below: Ivatt Class 2 2-6-2T No. 41284 at Edlington(Edlington for Balby to give its full title) with the Dearne Valley auto-train on 18th August 1951. *Neville Stead collection*

Above: Even this scene on the still active South Yorkshire Joint line is now a railway memory as the Class 58s have all been withdrawn. No. 58003 approaches Dinnington with empties for Maltby or Harworth colliery on 7th July 1998. The trees on the right of the line to the back of the train mark the site of Anston Junction but most of the old Midland & Great Central joint line to Laughton West Junction, closed in the 1920s, has disappeared under the plough. *Stephen Chapman*

Brancliffe East to Braithwell Junction was listed in the Eastern Region 1969 Sectional Appendix as a goods line worked by Permissive Block to Dinnington Colliery Jn., then a goods line worked by Absolute Block to Thurcroft Sidings and then a passenger line worked by Absolute Block to Braithwell Jn.

Signal boxes with distances from previous boxes were at Dinnington Colliery Junction(3 miles 631 yds from Brancliffe Jn.,) Thurcroft Sidings(2 miles 159yds,) Hellaby(2 miles 463yds,) and Braithwell Junction(1704yds.) The maximum line speed was 25mph.

The South Yorkshire Joint from Dinnington Colliery Junction to St. Catherine's Junction(Doncaster) was classed as a goods line with Absolute Block signalling from Dinnington Colliery Jn. to Dinnington station and Electric Token thereafter.

Signal boxes with distances from previous boxes, were at: Dinnington(1606yds from Dinnington Colliery Junction,) Maltby(4 miles 1056yds,) Maltby Colliery South(912yds,) Maltby Colliery North(532yds,) Firbeck Junction "A"(1 mile 1034yds,) Tickhill(1 mile 202 yds,) and St. Catherine's Junction(2miles 1263yds.)

Maximum line speed was 25mph. Crossing loops were provided at Firbeck Junction "A," and Tickhill station(until 1970) where there were also Up and Down refuge sidings.

Firbeck Junction "A" to Harworth Colliery is 4 miles 32 yds and was shown by the 1969 Sectional Appendix to be a goods line

worked by Train Staff and Ticket with a maximum line speed of 15mph.The Sectional Appendix also stated: "The single line between Firbeck "B" Harworth Junction ground frame hut, Harworth Colliery and Firbeck Colliery, is controlled by Key Token working in accordance with Electric Token Block regulations." The Harworth and Firbeck colliery empty sidings branches, also 15mph line speed, were worked according to "One Engine in Steam" regulations, the Firbeck Train Staff being kept in the Firbeck Colliery shunter's cabin. The Harworth Train Staff was round and lettered "Harworth Colliery Box and Colliery" and fitted with an Annetts Key for operating points to the NCB empty wagon sidings.

The above cannot adequately explain the working of these colliery branches as train crew and signallers had to be familiar with three pages of complicated instructions in the Sectional Appendix!

Braithwell Junction to Bullcroft Junction was still listed in the Sectional Appendix for 1969. It was classed as a passenger line worked by Absolute Block. The were no intermediate signal boxes between Braithwell Junction and Warmsworth Junction 4 miles 1241yds away where it connected with a branch from Yorkshire Main Colliery. The maximum line speed was given as 25mph. A special instruction stated: "Freight trains only - passenger trains to use this line only on authority of the Movements Manager." The line was deleted from the Sectional Appendix in a supplement issued on 4th may 1970.

Above: WD 2-8-0 No. 90108 plods through Dinnington & Laughton station with a 1950s Doncaster-bound coal train. The station has been officially closed since 1929 but the platforms remain in good condition for the occasional excursion train. *Neville Stead colln.*
The 1956 Stations Handbook listed Dinnington & Laughton as able to handle parcels and all classes of freight except carriages and motor cars by passenger or parcels train. There was no permanent crane. Goods facilities were withdrawn on 3rd May 1965. Private sidings served the East Midlands Gas Board gas works(prominent in the picture,) and the NCB's Dinnington Main Colliery and coke ovens.

Below: An unidentified Brush Type 2 trundles through the much reduced station with a late 1960s class 8 goods conveying what appear to be scrap sleepers. Dinnington station signal box, just visible at the platform end, was abolished in 1973. *Adrian Booth*

Above: The Dinnington-Thurcroft Sidings section of line survived until 1991 to serve Thurcroft Colliery. This was the scene in the colliery yard on 3rd April 1968 when Hunslet-built Austerity 0-6-0ST No. 5(works No. 3182/44) was the pit's only loco. The random collection of wagons on the left adds an extra dimension in terms of fascination. *Adrian Booth*

SHORT MEMORIES

24-28.2.72: A reduction in traffic and power cuts during the first miners' national strike since 1926 lead to the MSW lines being diesel worked and the Class 76s placed in temporary store.The Worsborough branch closes completely until 23rd February when it reopens for the passage of special electrically-hauled coal trains from Scotland to Lancashire power stations.

6 & 9.6.72: Class 44 "Peaks" Nos. 9 *Snowdon* and 10 *Tryfan* respectively pass Mexborough on iron ore specials to Scunthorpe.

30.12.80: 76006, assisted by 76054 to Barnsley Jn., take the LCGB's Xmas Tommy railtour up the Worsborough bank.

Summer 1986: The Advanced Passenger Train is broken up at C.F. Booth's.

May 1987: Many services using the new Rotherham Central station temporarily diverted to Masborough because, it is alleged, crew training is not complete.

One train working Dinnington Colliery box to Thurcroft Sidings. Except in an emergency, the Arrival line must only be used for trains travelling to Thurcroft Colliery sidings and the Local line for trains travelling from Thurcroft Colliery sidings.

When, in emergency, either line is to be used as a single line, drivers will be advised of the circumstances and must act in accordance with the instructions given to them by the signalman at Dinnington Colliery box. *Supplement to Eastern Region 1969 Sectional Appendix issued 4th May 1970.*

Rail traffic ceased at Dinnington in December 1985 with coal being taken by road to Thurcroft preparation plant. Thurcroft itself closed in December 1991.

Below: Steam had given way to diesel at Thurcroft by the end of the 1960s and the colliery's one loco became ex-BR Drewry Class 04 0-6-0 No. D2334, withdrawn from Darlington depot in 1968 and sent to Thurcroft, via Manvers Main, in 1969. It is seen up on blocks for attention outside the delightful loco shed on 8th March 1978. *Adrian Booth*

Above: Maltby station. still very much complete on 11th May 1952, and receiving an excursion in the form of a RCTS railtour hauled by B1 4-6-0 No. 61166. *Lance Brown/Neville Stead collection*

Below: WD 2-8-0 No. 90636 manoeuvres its train at Maltby Colliery sidings. In 2009 Maltby is the last active pit on the South Yorkshire Joint. *Neville Stead collection*

Right: Maltby Colliery South signal box on 8th February 1979. By the end of the 20th century almost the entire South Yorkshire Joint and the Harworth branch were controlled by this surviving box at Maltby, interfacing with Worksop just north of Dinnington and Doncaster at Tickhill.
Adrian Booth

Below: Class 58 No. 58015 heads towards the former Harworth Junction on the Harworth Colliery branch with a loaded MGR train at 15.35 on 31st March 1998.
Stephen Chapman

Above: Firbeck Junction "B" signal box on 2nd September 1978
Adrian Booth

Trains travelling from Firbeck Junction "B" to Harworth Colliery must obtain a Token from the signalman at Firbeck Junction "B" box lettered "Firbeck Junction 'B' and Firbeck Colliery" and on arrival at Harworth Junction the guard or secondman must proceed to the ground frame hut and advise the signalman at Harworth Colliery, by telephone, of his arrival. The Harworth Colliery signalman will then release the Auxiliary instrument to enable a Token lettered Harworth Junction-Harworth Colliery" to be obtained...*Eastern Region Sectional Appendix 1969*

INDUSTRIALS

Above: A mouthwatering selection of saddletanks at the NCB's Manvers Main loco shed on 6th June 1969. The engines are Hunslet-built Austerity 0-6-0STs Nos. 65(3889 of 1964,) 48(3685 of 1948,) and 51 *Raymond*(3834 of 1955,) Yorkshire Engine Co. 0-6-0ST No. 11(1823 of 1922,) and Peckett 0-6-0ST No.44 *Wilf*(1891 of 1940.)
Around this time Manvers Main(excluding the coke works) had 18 locomotives on its books of which 12 were steam, seven of those being either out of use or derelict.

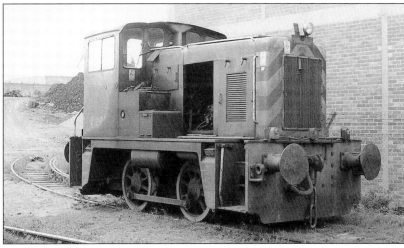

Bottom: Manvers' No.11(Yorkshire Engine Co. 1823/22) still game at the loco shed on 11th June 1968.

Centre: A Yorkshire Engine Co. product of a very different kind. This one is ex-BR 170hp Class 02 0-4-0 diesel hydraulic No. D2854 which was works shunter at C.F. Booth's in Rotherham when photographed on 12th September 1980.
Withdrawn from Allerton depot, Merseyside, in 1970, D2854 went to Booth's in the same year.
All Adrian Booth

109

Above: As with Manvers, Houghton Main Colliery, just up the North Midland line, could also sport a varied assortment of locomotives. The line-up of 0-6-0STs there on 8th September 1951 shows, from right: Hawthorn Leslie No. 3899 of 1936, Peckett 1303 of 1913, Hunslet Austerity No. 3178 of 1944(ex-WD No. 75128,) and Peckett No. 1519 of 1919. *Neville Stead collection*

Below: This Beyer Peacock 0-6-0ST at Treeton Colliery was curiously named *Rothervale No.0*. It was cut up three month after Neville Stead photographed it on 18th July 1959.

Above: A selection of Yorkshire Engine Co. locos at the British Steel Corporation's Templeborough works, formerly Steel Peach & Tozer, on 13th May 1979.

The 0-4-0 on the left is No.2 *Rotherham*. It was the first diesel built by the Yorkshire Engine Co. when turned out in 1950, works No. 2480. It was preserved in 1987.

Right: One of the more unusual industrial railways - this monorail at Mexborough sewage works, seen on 25th November 1980.

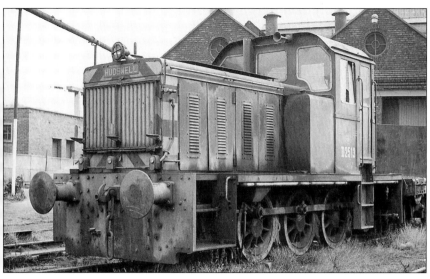

Left: Outside the loco shed at Cadeby Main Colliery on 6th December 1974 was ex-BR D2513, a Hudswell Clarke 204hp 0-6-0 diesel mechanical shunter. Withdrawn in 1967 from Barrow shed, it was scrapped around October 1975. *All pictures on this page by Adrian Booth*

Above: These locos in the yard at Silverwood Colliery on 11th June 1978 rarely saw the light of day, being narrow gauge locos built by English Electric/Baguley Drewry for working exclusively underground. Electrically powered from an overhead trolley wire, they had just been brought to the surface after 10 years out of use, pantographs removed. They were rebuilt by GEC Traction and put back to work at a pit in the North East. On the left is standard gauge Hudswell Clarke 0-6-0 D1138/1958 - very much a surface loco. Regular use of standard gauge surface locos ceased in 1981 when a rapid loading bunker came into operation. *Adrian Booth*

Left: The exquisite Yorkshire Engine Co. 0-6-0T *Hepworth*, works No. 799 of 1905, at the Hepworth Iron Company's Crow Edge works, near Hazlehead.
Neville Stead collection

112